주한미군지위협정(SOFA)

한·미
합동위원회 4

주한미군지위협정(SOFA)

한·미 합동위원회 4

한국학술정보

| 머리말

미국은 오래전부터 우리나라 외교에 있어서 가장 긴밀하고 실질적인 우호 · 협력관계를 맺어 온 나라다. 6 · 25전쟁 정전 협정이 체결된 후 북한의 재침을 막기 위한 대책으로서 1953년 11월 한미 상호방위조약이 체결되었다. 이는 미군이 한국에 주둔하는 법적 근거였고, 그렇게 주둔하게 된 미군의 시설, 구역, 사업, 용역, 출입국, 통관과 관세, 재판권 등 포괄적인 법적 지위를 규정하는 것이 바로 주한미군지위협정(SOFA)이다. 그러나 이와 관련한 협상은 계속된 난항을 겪으며 한미 상호방위조약이 체결로부터 10년이 훌쩍 넘은 1967년이 돼서야 정식 발효에 이를 수 있었다. 그럼에도 당시 미군 범죄에 대한 한국의 재판권은 심한 제약을 받았으며, 1980년대 후반 민주화 운동과 함께 미군 범죄 문제가 사회적 이슈로 떠오르자 협정을 개정해야 한다는 목소리가 커지게 되었다. 이에 1991년 2월 주한미군지위협정 1차 개정이 진행되었고, 이후에도 여러 사건이 발생하며 2001년 4월 2차 개정이 진행되어 현재에 이르고 있다.

본 총서는 외교부에서 작성하여 최근 공개한 주한미군지위협정(SOFA) 관련 자료를 담고 있다. 1953년 한미 상호방위조약 체결 이후부터 1967년 발효가 이뤄지기까지의 자료와 더불어, 이후 한미 합동위원회을 비롯해 민 · 형사재판권, 시설, 노무, 교통 등 각 분과위원회의 회의록과 운영 자료, 한국인 고용인 문제와 관련한 자료, 기타 관련 분쟁 자료 등을 포함해 총 42권으로 구성되었다. 전체 분량은 약 2만 2천여 쪽에 이른다.

2024년 3월

한국학술정보(주)

| 일러두기

· 본 총서에 실린 자료는 2022년 4월과 2023년 4월에 각각 공개한 외교문서 4,827권, 76만 여 쪽 가운데 일부를 발췌한 것이다.

· 각 권의 제목과 순서는 공개된 원본을 최대한 반영하였으나, 주제에 따라 일부는 적절히 변경하였다.

· 원본 자료는 A4 판형에 맞게 축소하거나 원본 비율을 유지한 채 A4 페이지 안에 삽입하였다. 또한 현재 시점에선 공개되지 않아 '공란'이란 표기만 있는 페이지 역시 그대로 실었다.

· 외교부가 공개한 문서 각 권의 첫 페이지에는 '정리 보존 문서 목록'이란 이름으로 기록물 종류, 일자, 명칭, 간단한 내용 등의 정보가 수록되어 있으며, 이를 기준으로 0001번부터 번호가 매겨져 있다. 이는 삭제하지 않고 총서에 그대로 수록하였다.

· 보고서 내용에 관한 더 자세한 정보가 필요하다면, 외교부가 온라인상에 제공하는 『대한민국 외교사료요약집』 1991년과 1992년 자료를 참조할 수 있다.

| 차례

정/리/보/존/문/서/목/록

기록물종류	문서-일반공문서철	등록번호	32962	등록일자	2009-03-30
분류번호	729.41	국가코드		주제	
문서철명	SOFA 한.미국 합동위원회 운영, 1982				
생산과	안보과	생산년도	1982 - 1982	보존기간	영구
담당과(그룹)	미주	안보	서가번호	--	
참조분류					
권차명					
내용목차					

마/이/크/로/필/름/사/항

촬영연도	*롤 번호	화일 번호	후레임 번호	보관함 번호

/

기안용지

분류기호 문서번호	미안 723-	(전화번호)	전결규정 조 항 전결사항
처리기간		장 관	
시행일자	82. 10. 12.		
보존년한			

보조기관			협조
차 관	전결		
국 장			
과 장			
기 안 책 임 자	김영훈	안 보 과	

경 유 / 수 신 / 참 조	수신처 참조	발신	통제
제 목	한·미 주둔군 지위협정 운영의 활성화		

한·미 주둔군 지위협정 (SOFA)의 시행을 위해 설치된 한·미 합동위원회는 각분과위원회 및 사무국과 더불어 협정발효후 지금까지 15년을 경과하면서 주한미군과 관련된 제반문제를 효과적으로 처리함으로써 한·미 양국간의 안보유대관계를 공고히 하는데 크게 기여하여 왔음은 사실이나 업무가 일상화함에 따라 관계부처의 관심도가 점점 저하하는 경향을 보이고 있는바, 귀부에서는 아래사항을 참고, 합동위원회 및 분과위원회 활성화에 적극협조하여 주시기 바랍니다.

- 아 래 -

1. 합동위원회 위원들이 합동위회의에 대리인을 참석시키거나 대리인조차 파견하지 않고 불참하는 경우가 많은바 SOFA 가 국민생활과 직접관련된 협정일 뿐만

/후면계속/

정서 | 관인 | 발송

0201 - 1 - 8 A(갑)
1969. 11. 10. 승인

정직 질서 창조

190mm×268mm (2급인쇄용지 60g/m²)
조 달 청 (3,000,000매 인 쇄)

아니라 자칫 미측에 대해 우리 정부의 무관심이란 인상을 줄 우려가 있는바 부득이한 경우를 제외하고는 위원들이 적극 회의에 참석토록 협조 바람.

2. 각분과위원회는 합동위원회가 부여한 과제에 대해서만 합동위에의 건의등 결정을 할 수 있으며 이를 위해서는 한.미 양측 분과위원회 위원들이 참석하는 회의를 소집하여야만 가능한바 어떤 분과위는 회의를 개최함이 없이 양측 분과위원장의 서명만 득하여 합동위원회에 건의를 제출하는등 과제처리절차를 이수하지 않고 있는바 반드시 소정의 절차를 거쳐 과제를 처리할 것이 요망됨.

3. 또한 대미교섭의 효율성 제고를 위해 각분과위원회 소집에 앞서 관련부처간의 긴밀한 사전협의가 필요할 것임.

4. 각분과위원회 (주관부처)는 미측으로부터 해당분과위에 관련된 문의나 정보를 접수하는 경우, 관련부처 및 합동위 한국측 사무국 (외무부 미주국 안보과)에 통보하여 주시고 특히 미측에 대한 회신의 경우 관련부처와 사전협의를 가짐으로써 업무상의 혼선을 방지하고 효과적인 대미교섭에 임할 수 있을 것임.

수신처 : 경제기획원장관(물가정책국장), 재무부장관(관세국장),

3

0201-1-43A(2-2)
1972. 12. 29. 승인
190mm×268mm(2급인쇄용지 60g/m²)
조달청(3,000,000매 인쇄)

법무부장관 (법무실장, 검찰국장, 출입국관리국장),

국방부장관(정책기획관, 시설국장),

상공부장관(통상진흥국장), 교통부장관(육운국장),

노동부장관(노정국장), 관세청장(지도국장).

4

대 한 민 국
외 무 부

미안 723- 720-2239 1982. 10. 13.

수신 수신처 참조

제목 한.미 주둔군 지위협정 운영의 활성화

한.미 주둔군 지위협정(SOFA)의 시행을 위해 설치된 한.미 합동위원회는 각분과위원회 및 사무국과 더불어 협정 발효후 지금까지 15년을 경과하면서 주한미군과 관련된 제반 문제를 효과적으로 처리함으로써 한.미 양국간의 안보 유대관계를 공고히 하는데 크게 기여하여 왔음은 사실이나 업무가 일상화함에 따라 관계부처의 관심도가 점점 저하하는 경향을 보이고 있는바, 귀부에서는 아래 사항을 참고, 합동위원회 및 분과위원회 활성화에 적극 협조하여 주시기 바랍니다.

-아 래-

1. 합동위원회 위원들이 합동위회의에 대리인을 참석시키거나 대리인 조차 파견하지 않고 불참하는 경우가 많은바 SOFA가 국민생활과 직접 관련된 협정일 뿐만아니라 자칫 미측에 대해 우리 정부의 무관심이란 인상을 줄 우려가 있는바 부득이한 경우를 제외하고는 위원들이 적극 회의에 참석토록 협조 바람.

2. 각분과위원회는 합동위원회가 부여한 과제에 대해서만 합동위에의 건의등 결정을 할 수 있으며 이를 위해서는 한.미 양측 분과위원회 위원들이 참석하는 회의를 소집하여야만 가능한바 어떤 분과위는 회의를 개최함이 없이 양측 분과위원장의 서명

/후면계속/

5

미안 723-   1982. 10. 13.

만 득하여 합동위원회에 건의를 제출하는 등 과제 처리절차를 이수하지 않고 있는 바 반드시 소정의 절차를 거쳐 과제를 처리할 것이 요망됨.

3. 또한 대미교섭의 효율성 제고를 위해 각분과위원회 소집에 앞서 관련부처간의 긴밀한 사전협의가 필요할 것임.

4. 각분과위원회 (주관부처)는 미측으로부터 해당분과위에 관련된 문의나 정보를 입수하는 경우, 관련부처 및 합동위 한국측 사무국 (외무부 미주국 안보과)에 통보하여 주시고 특히 미측에 대한 회신의 경우 관련부처와 사전 협의를 가짐으로써 업무상의 혼선을 방지하고 효과적인 대미교섭에 임할 수 있을 것임.   끝.

외 무 부 장 관

정부 공문서 규정 제27조 제2항의 규정에 의하여
외 무 부 차 관 노 재 원 전결

수신처 : 경제기획원장관 (물가정책국장), 재무부장관 (관세국장),
법무부장관 (법무실장, 검찰국장, 출입국관리국장),
국방부장관 (정책기획관, 시설국장),
상공부장관 (통상진흥국장), 교통부장관(육운국장),
노동부장관 (노정국장), 관세청장 (지도국장).

6

공 란

공　　　란

공 란

공 란

공 란

공 란

공　　　　　　란

공 란

공 란

공 란

공 란

공　　　란

공 란

공 란

공 란

공 란

공　　란

공 란

공 란

공 란

공 란

공 란

공 란

공　　　란

공 란

공 란

공 란

공 란

공　　　란

공　　란

공 란

공 란

공 란

공 란

공 란

공　　　　란

공 란

공 란

공 란

공 란

공　　　란

공 란

공 란

공 란

공　　　란

공 란

공 란

공 란

공 란

공 란

공 란

공 란

공 란

공　　　란

공 란

공 란

공 란

공 란

공 란

공 란

공　　란

공 란

공 란

공　　　란

공 란

공 란

공 란

공 란

공　　란

공 란

공 란

공 란

공 란

공 란

공 란

공 란

공 란

공 란

공 란

공　　란

공 란

공 란

공 란

공　　란

공 란

공　　　란

공 란

공 란

공 란

공 란

공　　　　란

공 란

공 란

공 란

공 란

공 란

공　　　란

공 란

공 란

공 란

공 란

공 란

공 란

공　　란

공 란

공 란

공 란

공 란

공 란

공 란

공 란

공 란

공 란

공 란

공 란

공 란

공 란

공　　란

공 란

공 란

공 란

공 란

공 란

공 란

공 란

공 란

공 란

공 란

공 란

공 란

공 란

공 란

공 란

공 란

공 란

공　　란

공 란

공 란

공 란

공 란

공 란

공　　　란

공　　란

공 란

공 란

공 란

공 란

공　　　란

공　　　란

공　　　란

공 란

공 란

공 란

공 란

공 란

공 란

공 란

공 란

공 란

공　　란

공 란

공 란

공 란

공 란

공　　　　란

공 란

공 란

공 란

공 란

정 리 보 존 문 서 목 록					
기록물종류	일반공문서철	등록번호	32964	등록일자	2009-03-30
분류번호	729.41	국가코드		보존기간	영구
명 칭	SOFA 한.미국 합동위원회 운영, 1985-86				
생 산 과	안보과	생산년도	1985~1986	담당그룹	북미국
내용목차					

기 안 용 지

분류기호 문서번호	미안 20294-	(전화번호)	전결규정 조 항 전결사항
처리기간	45623	장 관	
시행일자	1985. 12. 6.		
보존연한			
보조기관 국 장	전결		협조
심의관			
과 장			
기 안 책 임 자	이종국	안 보 과	
경 유			통제
수 신	수신처 참조	발송 1985.12.07 외무부	검열 1985.12.
참 조	SOFA 각 분과위원장		
제 목	SOFA 협정 운영상의 문제점 파악		

1. 주한미군의 지위에 관한 SOFA 협정에 따라 주한미군과 발생하는 모든 문제는 동 협정 제28조에 의거, 한미합동위원회를 통하여 협의, 해결하도록 되어 있으며 동 합동위원회는 분야별로 분과위원회를 구성하여 해당 분과 위원회에 과제를 부여, 처리하고 있읍니다.

2. 최근 일부 부처에서는 SOFA 합동위원회를 경유하지 않고 관계부처간의 충분한 협의를 거치지도 않은 채 미측에 문제를 제기하여 혼선이 야기되는 사례가 있는바, 앞으로는 주한미군과 발생하는 모든문제는 동 합동위를 통하여 관계부처간의 충분한 협의를 거쳐 아측입장을 결정한후 일관성 있게 미군측과 협의하는 것이 필요할 것으로 사료됩니다.

3. 또한 일부 분과위원회에서는 소관업무에 대한 이해와

정서 / 관인 / 발송

0001

/뒷면계속/

1205-25(2-1) A (갑) 1981. 12. 18승인

정직 질서 창조

190mm×268mm (인쇄용지 2급 60g/㎡) 가 40-41 1985. 8. 7.

문제해결이 지연되고

관심부족으로 ~~문제의제기나 해결을 회피하여 아국의 국위를 손상시키고 국민의 주한미군에 대한 불신감을 조성하여~~ 한미관계에 불필요한 오해를 야기하는 사례~~가 있다고 사료되는 바~~도 있는바, 각분과위원회에서는 소관업무에 대한 철저한 이해를 가지고 SOFA협정에 따라 모든 문제가 원활히 해결되도록 하여야 할것~~입니다~~이 요망되고 있습니다.

4. 이와관련하여 현재 각분과위원회에서 파악하고 있는 SOFA 관련, 현안문제점을 파악하고자 하오니 이를 당부에 통보하여 주시기 바랍니다. (당부에 기통보된 내용은 제외). 끝.

수신 : 경제기획원장관(물가정책국장), 법무부장관(법무실장, 검찰국장, 출입국관리국장) 국방부장관(정책기획관, 시설국장), 재무부장관(관세국장), 노동부장관(노정국장), 상공부장관(통상진흥국장), 교통부장관(육운국장), 관세청장(지도국장).

0002

韓國人종업원에 竊盜혐의 美軍부대 懸賞벽보 말썽

釜山·大邱·倭館등서 부대안에 붙여놔

"人權모독이다" 항의

지난5월 勞組파업에 報復인상 짙어

釜山·大邱·倭館등 일부지역의 美軍부대에서 물품의 도난이나 부정유출을 막는다는 구실로 현상금을 건다는 美軍부대근무 韓國人 근로자들의 인권을 침해하는 내용의 벽보를 붙여놓아 반발을 사고있다.

美육군 범죄수사사령부(USACIC)명의로된 이 벽보는 「사례금」이란 제목아래 「美합중국 정부재산을 절취하거나 유용한 자(들)에 관한 신원을 파악할수 있는 정보나 도난품 혹은 유용된 물건을 회수할수 있는 정보를 제공하는 자에게 美육군범죄수사사령부에서 사례금을 제공합니다」는 내용으로 7월초부터 부대안 사무실·복도등의 게시판에 붙여놓고 있다.

이 벽보가 나붙자 韓國人근로자들은 벽보내용에 韓國人근로자에게 협의를 둔 명시적인 표현은 없으나 韓國人근로자 전체를 모독하고 인권을 침해하는 처사라고 비난, 벽보의 즉각 철거를 美軍당국에 요구했으나 아직 벽보가 철거되지않고 있다.

◇사례금 벽보=가로50㎝, 세로 70㎝크기의 노랑·빨강·파랑등 3종류의 색종이에 쓰여진 이 벽보는 정보제공자의 신원에 관해 절대로 비밀을 보장하겠다고 약속하고 「사례금 제공은 86년9월30일까지 유효합니다」고 밝히고 있다.

◇항의·반발=大邱지방 美軍부대의 韓國人 근로자들은 이같은 벽보가 지난5월29일 노조원감원과 임금인상문제등을 내세워 駐韓美軍노조(위원장 姜賓植)조합원 2만4천여명이 파업을 벌인지 한달만에 게시됐다는 점을 들어 보복조치인상이 짙다고 판단, 노조본부를 통해 지난8월 美軍당국에 항의했으나 받아들여지지 않았다.

倭館지방 미군부대의 韓國人근로자들은 미군당국의 행정력이나 보안요원, 고성능 전자감시장치만으로도 물품도난이나 부정유출을 충분히 방지할수 있음에도 韓國人근로자의 자존심에 상처를 주는 이같은 벽보를 붙인것은 납득할수 없는 일이라고 주장하고 있으며 釜山지방 미군부대의 韓國人근로자들은 벽보가 철거되지 않은 상태에서 지난9월초 미군수사당국이 PX근무자의 몸수색을 철저히 하라는 새로운 보안지침을 PX관리자들에게 시달했다며 韓國人근로자들을 범죄인시하는 미군당국에 불만을 표시하고 있다.

駐韓美軍부대의 韓國人근로자는 전국적으로 3만여명이며 이가운데 6천여명은 비노조원이다. 龍山·平澤·烏山·議政府지방의 미군부대에는 이같은 벽보가 붙지않은 것으로 확인됐다.

◇姜賓植駐韓미군노조위원장=8월초 釜山지부의 보고를 받고 미8군인사담당자에게 한차례 비공식 항의를 했었다. 釜山지방등에 아직 벽보가 붙어있다면 즉시 철거하도록 조치하겠다.

◇駐韓미군 공보담당자=도난 혹은 유용된 美정부재산을 회수하고 같은 종류의 범죄를 예방하기 위해 벽보를 붙였다. 駐韓미군 노조로부터 항의를 받은 일도 없으며 韓國人근로자들이 반발할 이유가 없다고 본다. PX책임자에게 관리를 철저히 하라고 지시한 일은 있으나 韓國人근로자의 몸수색을 강화하라고 시달한 일은 없다.

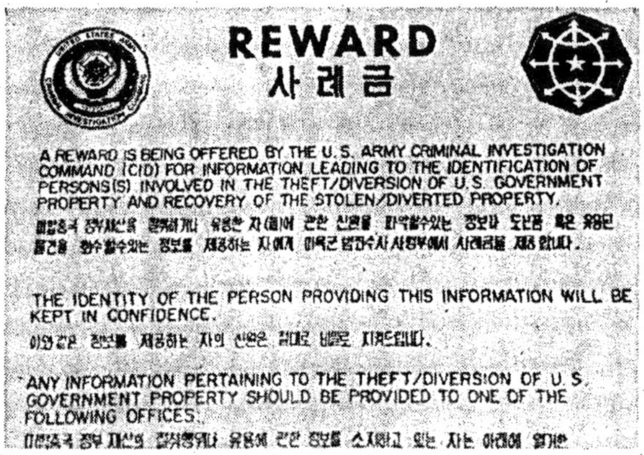

REWARD
사례금
A REWARD IS BEING OFFERED BY THE U.S. ARMY CRIMINAL INVESTIGATION COMMAND (CID) FOR INFORMATION LEADING TO THE IDENTIFICATION OF PERSONS(S) INVOLVED IN THE THEFT/DIVERSION OF U.S. GOVERNMENT PROPERTY AND RECOVERY OF THE STOLEN/DIVERTED PROPERTY.
THE IDENTITY OF THE PERSON PROVIDING THIS INFORMATION WILL BE KEPT IN CONFIDENCE.
ANY INFORMATION PERTAINING TO THE THEFT/DIVERSION OF U.S. GOVERNMENT PROPERTY SHOULD BE PROVIDED TO ONE OF THE FOLLOWING OFFICES.

문제의 벽보 미군부대안에 붙여진 현상금벽보。「사례금」이란 제목으로 물품절취·유용등 정보를 제공하는 사람에게는 사례금을 준다고 적혀있다。

0003

형사재판권
민사재판권

GI tried in S. Korea killing

CAMP FOSTER, Japan (PS&S) — Lance Cpl. Robert D. Pounds, one of two Marines charged with the shooting death in November of a South Korean woman near Seoul, went before a general court-martial here Monday, according to a Marine Corps spokesman.

Pounds and Pfc. Mark T. Kerns, both assigned to the 12th Marine Regiment, have been charged with manslaughter and assault, the spokesman said. Kerns' trial will begin Feb. 4, he said.

The incident occurred Nov. 8 along a highway north of Seoul as Pounds, Kerns and another Marine were en route by truck to pick up ammunition, according to a statement issued by U.S. Forces Korea. The Marines were taking part in an annual training exercise, the command said.

An M-16 rifle carried by one of the men discharged, the statement said, and a bullet struck and killed the woman who Korean authorities identified as Kim Yong Ja, 44.

The Marine spokesman on Okinawa said the assault charge is based on "alleged actions within a moving vehicle during which both Marines allegedly pointed and fired M-16 weapons with blank ammunition without regard for safety and regulations."

In a November report concerning Pounds' arrest, South Korea's Yonhap News Agency said the Marine "had intended to pick up blank ammunition from a box, but he mistakenly took real ammunition from another box."

성조지. 86. 2. 5.

0004

공　　란

공 란

공 란

공 란

공 란

공 란

공 란

공 란

공 란

공　　　란

공　　　란

공 란

공　　란

공 란

기 안 용 지

분류기호 문서번호	미안 20294- 1248 (전화번호)	전결규정 조 항 전결사항	
처리기간		장 관	
시행일자	1986. 5. 19.		
보존연한			

보조기관	국 장	전 결	협조
	심의관		
	과 장		
기안책임자	손성환	안 보 과	

경유 수신 참조	내무부장관, 법무부장관 치안국장, 출입국관리국장	발신 (반수성 1986. 5. 20 외무부)	통제 (검열 1986. 5. 20 통제관)
제목	미8군 한미 문화교류 협회 영어 강좌		

1. 미8군 한미 문화교류 협회 (KASA) 는 86.5.12.자 중앙일보 및 일간 스포츠에 별첨과 같이 미8군 영내에서 영어교습을 실시할 것임을 광고하였으며 동 광고 내용중에는 KASA 회원은 미8군 영내 각종 시설물 이용권을 부여한다고 허위 광고하고 있읍니다.

2. 한.미 주둔군 지위협정 (SOFA) 에 의하면 주한미군, 군속 및 가족등은 주둔목적이외의 영리행위를 금지하고 있으며 미8군 영내의 각종면세 시설물 (비세출자금 기관)은 SOFA협정대상자 이외에는 한국 정부의 명시적 동의가 없는한 이용할 수 없도록 되어 있는바, 상기 KASA 광고는 SOFA 협정에 위배되는 사항입니다. 이와관련, 주한 미군 당국은 5.14.자로 동 광고가 허위라는 별첨과 같은 성명을 발표 한바 있읍니다.

정서 / 관인 / 발송

0019

1205-25(2-1)A(갑) 1981. 12. 18승인

정직 질서 창조

190㎜×268㎜(인쇄용지 2급 60g/㎡) 가 40-41 1985. 8. 7.

3. 상기와 같은 주한미군을 빙자한 허위 광고에 대하여 조사, 의법조치 하여 주시고 그 결과를 당부에도 통보하여 주시기 바랍니다.

첨부 : 1. 미8군 한미 문화 교류협회 광고

2. 주한미군 당국 발표문. 끝.

0020

ENGLISH SCHOOL 개강안내

본 English School에서는 KASA STAFF의 후원을 얻어 영어를 필요로 하는 모든 분들을 위한 어학 Seminar Program을 기초부터 단계적으로 다음과 같이 실시하오니 많은 참여를 바랍니다.

○내 용 : English Seminar Program
○모집대상 : 고졸이상의 직장인, 일반인, 대학생, 주부
(성별 연령 제한이 없으며 기초가 없는 분도 가능함)
○연수기간 : 1986년 6월16일~11월30일

Time schedule

월, 화반	목, 금반	토, 일반
A. 10 : 30~12 : 30	D. 10 : 30~12 : 30	G. 13 : 00~15 : 00
B. 17 : 00~19 : 00	E. 17 : 00~19 : 00	H. 15 : 00~17 : 00
C. 19 : 30~21 : 30	F. 19 : 30~21 : 30	I. 17 : 00~19 : 00

※월·목·토 교육 : 발음교정→기초회화→응용회화 (한국인교수)
※화·금·일 교육 : 소규모 meeting Room에서의 Free talking 및 INTERVIEW(Room별 전원 외국인교수)

○연수장소 : 1. KASA 빌딩(미8군옆 삼각지 소재)
2. 미8군 영내에서의 현장학습
○연수비용 : 본 연수과정은 미8군의 후원으로 운영되므로 교육비는 면제받으며 교육자료비만 본인이 부담합니다.
교육자료. 교재 7권 Self Study용 Lap Tape 26개로 매월 20,000원씩 6회로 6개월간 분납(합계 120,000원)

★ English School Member 특전 ★

☆본 English School의 모든 Member는 전원 미8군 KASA 회원으로 정식 가입됩니다.
☆KASA 회원은 한,미 생활관 및 미국인 회원과의 개별적인 Meeting을 통하여 미국사회에서 사용빈도가 높은 언어세계를 익힐 수 있읍니다.
☆KASA 회원은 미8군 영내의 각종 시설물(극장, 수영장, 보링장, Resturant 각종 Club 및 기타 오락시설)을 이용할 수 있으며 KASA의 정기 Program(각종 Party, Meeting Picnic)에 정식 Member로써 참여합니다.
☆KASA는 현재 AFKN-TV에서 안내방송예정입니다.

○접수방법 : 각반 선착순 관계로 서울, 경기지역은 전화로 접수함.
5월12일~14일한, 접수된 회원에게는 3일이내로 모든 KASA Program과 연수자료가 자택이나 직장으로 도착되며 도착시 1회분 20,000원과 KASA 회원용 증명사진 2매를 준비하여 주시기 바랍니다.

○접 수 처 : 직통전화 797-3121, 3122, 3105

미8군 한미문화 교류협회
KOREAN AMERICAN SOCIAL ASSOCIATION

0021

News Release

Public Affairs

CFC, Historian

UNITED NATIONS COMMAND / COMBINED FORCES COMMAND
UNITED STATES FORCES KOREA / EIGHTH UNITED STATES ARMY

APO 96301
TEL: 3113/3290

RELEASE NUMBER: 5-11/dlm

KASA "ENGLISH SCHOOL" NOT AFFILIATED WITH USFK

SEOUL (U.S. Forces Korea), May 14, 1986 -- Eighth U.S. Army officials today said a recent advertisement in local newspapers concerning an English School at Yongsan Army Garrison and the Samgak-ji area was fraudulently false. "Eighth Army has no connection with this so-called school or an English Seminar Program," a spokesman emphasized.

The advertisement was taken out by the Korean American Social Association (KASA), an unofficial social organization, and appeared earlier this week in two Seoul newspapers.

The spokesman pointed out that KASA is not sanctioned by Eighth Army for creation of a school or for the use of its name.

He said that KASA has not even requested permission from Eighth Army to use any facilities at Yongsan Military Reservation for study purposes and students would not be eligible, under the Republic of Korea/United States Status of Forces Agreement, to use any other Eighth Army facilities such as theaters, swimming pools, etc., contrary to what the ad promised.

"We have no knowledge of anyone authorizing the use of Eighth Army's name in conjunction with this English School," the spokesman said. "We sincerely regret any inconvenience or

0022

-more-

KASA "ENGLISH SCHOOL" NOT AFFILIATED WITH USFK
2-2-2-2-2-2-2-2-2-2-2-2-2-2-2-2-2-2-2-2-2-2-2

embarrassment this fraudulent advertisement may have caused individuals who attempted to enroll."

Neither Eighth Army nor U.S. Forces Korea have authorized the use of their names or emblems in conjunction with the KASA English School.

"Eighth Army has requested local authorities to investigate the deceptive advertisment," he added.

-30-

0023

CHIEF OF STAFF
USFK/EUSA

CO, 501st SG
PAJ
JAJ
} cy each

Get on w/ disclaimer ASAP _ PAJ (coord w/ JAJ)

Evaluate status of KASA as Private Orgn ASAP - 501st SG (coord w/ JAJ).

Keep SOFA, (Dr Hodges) informed of all actions.

Ellis
14 May

HQ USFK FORM 20, 1 Feb 82

0024

• Memorandum

Public Affairs Office

UNITED NATIONS COMMAND / COMBINED FORCES COMMAND
UNITED STATES FORCES KOREA / EIGHTH UNITED STATES ARMY

APO SF 96301
TEL: 293-3965

14 May 1986

USFK C/S ~~CofS~~ See note - [illegible]

You need to be aware of the attached. I have notified COL Spiller and have asked SJA for an opinion on whether PAO should run a disclaimer.

If this is as it appears, an attempt to rip the Koreans off, with promises of on post privileges under the guise of EUSA sponsorship the potential problems are many.

Also raises the question of other quasi official organizations out there doing their own thing. - 501st should review all of them.

VR

[signature]

FREDDIE J. USSERY
LTC, USA
Public Affairs Officer

0025

Copy

PAJ Review of Korean American Social Association

JAJ
ATTN: Col Morrow/

Public Affairs Office
USFK/EUSA

14 May 1986
MAJ Morrison/llm/3965

1. The attached advertisement was published in the Korean language "Joong Ang Newspaper" and the "Daily Sports Newspaper" 12 May 1986. It may have also run in other newspapers we're not aware of. A rough translation is provided from one of our Korean writers.

2. CSM Clayton, 18th Medical Command, is the co-chairman of the American participants in this organization. The Korean American Social Association (KASA) is indeed a private organization authorized to meet on post. However, CSM Clayton stated that he was not aware of the advertisement nor the existence of the English School. He stated that Mr. Lee, the head of the organization, had been told not to publicize anything without the approval of the Community Affairs Division. There is in fact no Eighth Army support for this English School. CSM Clayton stated he did not wish to be associated with this organization any longer and questioned whether they should be allowed on post.

3. CPT Hoffman, Chief of the 501st Support Group Community Affairs Division, agreed that the KASA was an authorized private organization; however the English School activity was not sanctioned by Eighth Army. She raised the question of having the organization disbanded as a private organization and having Mr. Lee barred from post, since this was just another of a series of unauthorized actions on his part.

4. We are wondering whether it would be appropriate for Eighth Army to publish a disclaimer in the Korean newspapers denying sponsorship or support for this English School. We do not want the Korean populace to be mislead or cheated in the name of Eighth Army. If you advise that this disclaimer would be appropriate, PAJ will prepare and release the disclaimer notice.

FREDDIE J. USSERY
LTC, USA
Public Affairs Officer

0028

* * *

The boycott campaign of the KBS-TV audience fees will be continuously launched, the campaign headquarters said yesterday, noting that the measures sought by the ruling camp are far from renovating the public television station systems.

The headquarters said that the law on KBS-TV should be rewritten at the earliest possible date to help it play its media role as a public television station.

The KBS-TV should refrain from reporting "biased" news and those programs aimed at safeguarding the incumbent government, the headquarters said in a statement.

Today's Forecast

Fair skies are forecast over the country. Morning lows will be two to three degrees lower and afternoon highs will be a little higher than yesterday's. Waves will be one and a half to three meters high.

Seoul, Kyonggi: Clear
8°C(46°F) / 20°C(68°F)
Chungchong: Clear
7°C(45°F) / 22°C(70°F)
Kangwon: Clear
9°C(48°F) / 23°C(72°F)
Cholla: Clear
10°C(50°F) / 23°C(72°F)
Kyongsang: Clear
10°C(50°F) / 24°C(75°F)
Cheju: Clear
13°C(56°F) / 20°C(68°F)

Water-borne epidemic diseases are usually transmitted through drinking

Ad on English School At Yongsan Found To Be Fraudulent

Eighth U.S. Army officials said yesterday that the advertisement in local newspapers concerning an English school at Yongsan was fraudulent.

"The Eighth Army has no connection with the so-called school or an English seminar program," a spokesman said. The advertisement was taken out by the Korean-American Social Association (KASA), an unofficial social organization.

KASA is not sanctioned by EUSA to use any facilities at Yongsan military reservation for study purposes, the spokesman said, adding that local authorities were requested to investigate the deceptive advertisement.

160 Educators to Be Cited

A total of 160 exemplary educators will be honored with medals and citations given by the government today on the occasion of observing the Fifth Teachers' Day.

Among the honorees will be *Prof.* Park Chung-hi of the National Fisheries University and Prof. Kim Chong-ki of Dong-A University, both in Pusan, who will be conferred with the Order of Civil Service Merit, Dongbaek Medals.

the class fees ... must be higher than those at language centers open now.

They argue, however, that it is not in the interest of the commercial institutes nor the students.

They said when and if foreigners are allowed to engage in the business directly, there will follow a massive swing of students seeking instruction at the institutes run by foreigners.

The operators of the foreign language institutes pointed to the fact that there are foreign lecturers hired by their institutes so that students can have the experience of learning foreign languages from native speakers.

They said the measure of allowing foreigners to directly run the foreign language institutes is "too much" in the favor of foreigners.

The government is studying a plan to permit foreigners to run foreign language institutes to help improve Koreans' competency in foreign languages as much as possible for the nation's progress.

Hong Appointed as Nat'l Unification Council Head

The Central Consultative Council for National Unification appointed Hong Sung-chul as its new chairman in a meeting of board of directors yesterday.

The former minister of home affairs succeeds Hyun Sung-jong who took the presidency of Hallim University.

T...
Chonn...
rally ...

2 ...

I...

Two ...
arreste...
ducing...
to leac...
tutes ...
They ...
total o...
throug...
three ...
tion sa...
the co...
charg...
Acc...
sang, ...
Indus...
plex, ...
nol, x...

5.15.

Just 20,000 miles and you're flying free
Join the people who know.
NORTHWEST OR

0027

uch as ethanol
ome 1.2 billion
cts to about 400
s and business
some big-name
Lucky-Goldstar
eutical Co. and
Co.
eoul Chemical,
ond largest of its
about 400 kinds
president Chong
200 million won
products under
akyu Pure Che-

ter Lee
Honor

Defense Lee Ki-
ded with the Le-
ench government
he promotion of
o countries.
to Korea Jean-
ted the medal to
at his residence in
or for promoting
tween the two na-
s the chairman of
aff between June

contract
cklist
ocal cos.

Defense contract
ut the world ar
ecting fraud, wast
ary spokesman said
. companies which
racts or otherwise
nment during con-
being identified for
sion, he said.
barments preclude
iving any solicita-
g business with the
der the Federal Ac
nd its supplements
integrity can be de
years.
USFK) contracting
d the Korean Minis-
istry concerning the
etermination.

g-jin picked
n of KSEF

ce and Engineerin
esterday elected Dr
ourth chairman.
d as minister of com-
ister of science and
Lee Chung-oh who
he president of the
titute of Science and
ruary.

leftist ideology books

The Seoul prosecution yesterday arrested Park Yun-bae, 29, director of a small printing shop, on suspicion of printing blacklisted books on leftist ideologies.

Park, an expellee of Seoul National University, set up the printing shop in May last year and published the Japanese edition of the "Bolsheviki and the Russian Revolution" last September at the request of Paik Chu-mun, 32, a law graduate of SNU.

He divided the book into three parts and printed 2,000 copies for each of the three, according to the prosecution.

The prosecution is seeking Paik.

Park is also suspected of planning to issue more than 30 different leftist-leaning books.

The Bolsheviki and the Russian Revolution, said to be an educational manual on authentic communism, is generally intended to praise Bolshevism and introduce the process of Russian revolution based on Nikolai Lenin's doctrine.

The prosecution said investigation is also under way to determine the source of the fund for the publication of the books and discover possible secret connections with other printing shops.

standard-bearers of national unification. If south Korean students call for North-Korea student talks, we will be willing to accept it."

Seoul to map out plans against air pollution

Seoul city government has decided to formulate short-term and long-term plans to reduce air pollution.

The city has recently awarded a contract to an environmental engineering team to survey condition and sources of air pollution and meteorological condition affecting air contamination, and to submit concrete steps to fight air pollution.

The short-term plan entails the city meeting its projected goal of reducing sulphuric acid gas contamination from present 0.056 ppm to 0.038 ppm by 1988.

The long-term plan will cover the years beyond 1988 when the city is to host the 1988 Olympics.

The city's five-year environmental preservation plan which began in 1982 has produced little positive result, city officials said.

and breaking windows.

Chonnam was one of about 33 colleges and universities where rallies and demonstrations were held during the day.

The Yonhap News Agency reported that the Chonnam students commenced the rally around 2:40 p.m., chanting anti-government and anti-U.S. slogans. They were dispersed by riot policemen who charged into the campus around 3:15 p.m., firing tear gas shells.

Some of the students moved into the main campus building and smashed windows with wooden bars and stones.

One of the students lowered a Saemaul (New Community) flag from the flag post of the building and instead hoisted a red flag which bore a slogan reading, "Let's remember the May revolution," apparently referring to the "Kwangju incident" on May 17, 1980.

Another group of students burned a sedan parked outside the campus.

In Seoul, demonstrations were held at 12 schools, including Seoul National University and Ewha Woman's University.

About 800 Ewha students held a rally after holding what they called "a ceremony for the proclamation of campus liberalization."

The reception desk at the Korean American Social Association (KASA) office in Yongsan seems to be brisk with language-course applicants yesterday. The Eighth U.S. Army said it has no connections with the KASA.
Korea Herald

8th U.S. Army disavows validity of local ads about English course on Yongsan compound

Eighth U.S. Army officials said yesterday that a recent advertisement in Korean newspapers concerning an English school at Yongsan Army Garrison and the Samgakji area was "fraudulently false."

"Eighth Army has no connection with this so-called school or an English seminar program," a spokesman emphasized.

The advertisement was taken out by the Korean American Social Association (KASA), an unofficial organization, and appeared earlier this week in two Seoul newspapers, he said.

The spokesman pointed out that KASA is not sanctioned by Eighth Army for creation of a school or for the use of its name.

The advertisement said the language program will be conducted from June 16 through Nov. 30 at the KASA building and inside the Yongsan compound.

It also said all students will be able to utilize various Eighth Army facilities, including theaters, swimming pools, bowling alleys and restaurants.

A female KASA clerk said she understands about 500 persons applied for the school since the advertisements were carried last Monday.

The spokesman said that KASA has not even requested permission from Eighth Army to use any facilities at Yongsan Military Reservation for study purposes and students would not be eligible, under the Republic of Korea-United States Status of Forces Agreement, to use any other Eighth Army facilities such as theaters, swimming pools, etc., contrary to what the ad promised.

"We have no knowledge of anyone authorizing the use of Eighth Army's name in conjunction with this English school," the spokesman said.

Model prisoners up for Buddha's Birthday parole

The government will free 769 exemplary prisoners this morning on the occasion of Buddha's Birthday which falls tomorrow, the Ministry of Justice announced yesterday.

It said all of those to be released are ordinary criminals, including 31 inmates at the juvenile reformatories.

Also included are 11 persons who have served more than 10 years in prison and 9? others who have passed state-run vocational skill tests.

Ministry officials said those found guilty of violating national security-related crimes are not included in the annual clemency.

0028

5.15

JOINT COMMITTEE
UNDER
THE REPUBLIC OF KOREA AND THE UNITED STATES
STATUS OF FORCES AGREEMENT

21 May 1986

Dear Mr. Han:

In reference to your letter concerning the fraudulent advertisement involving English schooling by the Korean American Social Association, I am pleased to inform you that according to an investigation by the base commander, no U.S. personnel were involved in the matter.

It is true that there was a private organization named the Korean American Social Association (with an office near Yongsan) which was recognized by the base commander. The Association head had an access pass. However, this pass and recognition have been withdrawn. The investigating officer found that none of the few American members knew about the English teaching scheme or the advertisements.

Respectfully,

CARROLL B. HODGES
US Joint Committee Secretary

Mr. HAN Tae Kyu
Republic of Korea
Joint Committee Secretary

공람	안보과	86년 5월 23일	담당	과장	심의관	국장

0029

Guidance to opening of ENGLISH SCHOOL

With the sponsorship of KASA staff English School is scheduled a seminar for the people whomever needed English lesson.

a. Content: English Seminar Program
b. Participants: Whoever has above high school (12 years) education.
c. Period: 16 June thru 30 Nov 86

d. Time Schedule

Mon & Tue	Thur & Fri	Sat & Sun

e. Place: 1. KASA Bldg (at Samkackji near 8th Army)
2. OJT in 8th Army post.

f. Cost: The cost of text book only will be paid by the participants and fee is exempted since this program is sponsored by the Eighth U.S. Army. Total 120,000 won will be paid in six times with monthly allotment of 20,000 won for the 7 text books and 26 Lap Tapes.

Privileges of English School Members

All members of Engish School will be automatically belong to 8th U.S. Army KASA regular member.

Members of KASA will be accustomed to American philosophy of living and alive American English thru the individual meeting with American members.

Members of KASA can use various 8th Army facilities such as theaters, swimming pools, bowling alleys, restaurants and clubs etc., and participate regular KASA programs such as parties, meetings and picnics.

Information on KASA is scheduled to be aired on AFKN-TV.

g. How to apply: Telephone registrations will be made in Seoul and Kyonggi-do area. First come first registered basis. Members register between 12-14 May will have text books and guidance of KASA programs delivered either to their homes or to their works within 3 days. Please have 20,000 won and 2 photos ready at the time of delivery of the above.

h. Tel: 797-3121/3122/3105

KOREAN AMERICAN SOCIAL ASSOCIATION

0030

JAJ-AL (PAJ/14 May 86)
SUBJECT: Review of Korean American Social Association

TO PAJ FM JAJ DATE 14 MAY 1986 CMT 2
MAJ Duffy/tjd/3628

1. We strongly recommend a press release be prepared stating that the recent advertisement is false and fraudulent.

a. The press release should specifically disclaim any Eighth Army sponsorship or connection with the English School or the Seminar Program. The release should also state that the English School has not even requested permission from Eighth Army for the use of any facilities for study purposes. Additionally, students are not permitted to use any other EUSA facilities such as the theatres, swimming pools and like MWR facilities.

b. Recommend you also contact CPT Hoffman to determine the approved purposes of the Korean American Social Association, its membership (particularly by Mr. Lee), and whether its charter has been withdrawn as a result of this incident. If KASA is solely a social or fraternal organization, the press release could advise that while the organization has been authorized for certain purposes, the organization has not sanctioned the creation of an English School and that Mr. Lee has furthermore acted without seeking the approval of KASA for the use of its name.

c. The release should also state that we have no knowledge of who authorized the use of Eighth Army's name and that we have requested local authorities investigate the illegal and deceptive advertisement.

2. Recommend the press release be coordinated with this office (JAJ-IA, LtCol Schumann, ext. 6353/6485) as we have also been following this matter and may have preliminary results of the Yongsan Police's investigation. Our office's translation of the article is enclosed for your information.

3. In any event, recommend the newspapers which published the advertisement be phoned and told of the deceptive nature of the advertisement and that Eighth Army has no connection with the English School.

FOR THE JUDGE ADVOCATE:

Thomas J. Duffy
THOMAS J. DUFFY
MAJ, JA
Acting Chief, Admin Law Division

3 Encls
1-2 nc
added 1 encl
3. Translation

2

0031

공 란

공 란

공 란

공 란

공 란

USFK INVESTIGATION REVEALS RAPE RUMOR FALSE

Student radicals have spread a rumor to the effect that United States soldiers or marines recently raped a school teacher in the town of Chechon, and that the teacher committed suicide shortly thereafter. This allegation was thoroughly investigated on 6 and 7 May 1986 by a US attorney who visited Chechon. He inquired into the allegation with the view that any US personnel determined to be responsible for such an act would be promptly brought to justice.

The attorney, a fully bilingual Korean-American, made extensive inquiries of city officials and persons of various occupations in town. He failed to find any evidence that such an incident ever took place, and concluded the rumor [redacted] to be totally groundless.

However, USFK officials are adamant in their desire to bring to justice any United States personnel who participate in violent crimes against Koreans. Persons having knowledge of any such acts should report them at once to Republic of Korea or USFK authorities. ~~Any person having knowledge of the alleged Chechon incident is asked to contact the USFK Office of the Judge Advocate at Seoul 793-2834, 793-1851, or Yongsan 293-6353.~~

0037

 Korea Herald

Man sought for using bogus W10,000 bills in buying calves

Fled with W4.34 mil. in cash after resale

KIMCHON (Yonhap) — Police are searching for a man in his early 30s who left 16 million won (about $18,000) in forged 10,000-won bills after buying a dozen calves from a farmer near this southeastern provincial city last Saturday.

The suspect resold the calves to a livestock broker immediately after buying them from the farmer and fled with 4.34 million won in "real money" he pocketed from the resale, police said yesterday.

Suspect's montage

The counterfeit bills were the most refined ever found in the country, according to the Government Printing and Mint Agency, which examined the fraudulent bills at the request of the police.

The agency said that the forged bills are believed to have been designed by a printing technician, who used a brush or drawing pen, and that they were printed with an offset printing machine.

According to police, the suspect, in dealing with the 45-year-old farmer, Kim Ahn-soo, presented himself as the manager of a canned food company in charge of waste water control. He told Kim that he would buy the calves as compensation for damages suffered by the farmers living near the factory.

Police distributed 100,000 copies of the suspect's montage throughout the country and posted a one million-won reward for the arrest of the suspect or clues leading to arrest.

Considering the substantial sum of money involved in the case and the fact that it seems to have been premeditated, police suspect that one or two others may have collaborated with the suspect in the sting operation.

Yonhap

The counterfeit 10,000 won bill (photo above) looks crude compared to the genuine one shown in the photo below.

U.S. Embassy denies GIs' attack on Korean women during exercise

The U.S. Embassy in Seoul yesterday "flatly and categorically" denied rumors of gang assault committed by American military personnel against two Korean women in the central part of the country during the recent "Team Spirit" exercise.

In the statement, the embassy said it had been aware that various versions of a leaflet containing statements extremely critical of the United States have been circulated among some student groups or posted on university campuses. "The language of that text was so extreme and inflammatory that the embassy assumed that most people who read it would not take any part of it seriously," it said.

One of the charges in the leaflet, however, seems to have gained credence among some people, it said.

The American Embassy has made inquiries with U.S. military authorities and the Korean police, and has determined that no such incident occurred, the statement said.

"The American Embassy flatly and categorically denies the charges concerning rape in the various versions of the leaflet, and suggests that the same malevolent political motivation reflected in the other parts of that text lay behind the rape charges," it said.

Sporadic rallies mar rites on 6th anniv. of Kwangju incident

KWANGJU (Yonhap) — Sporadic demonstrations Sunday marked the sixth anniversary of the civil uprising here six years ago.

However, clashes between police and demonstrators were not too serious.

A total of 260 demonstrators were taken away by police, but all except six were released yesterday. Of the six, three were held for further investigation and three others were sent to a summary court trial.

Memorial services were held at the Kuwoldong cemetery at 10:30 a.m. with the participation of about 800 persons, including families of those who lost their lives in the "Kwangju incident," students and members of opposition organizations.

The ceremony was momentarily interrupted by disturbances created by about 50 members of a "Democratic Youth Movement." More than 100 local and foreign newsmen, including those from ABC and CBS TV networks, covered the rites.

The disturbances occurred as the "Democratic Youth Movement" members shouted catcalls and slogans against the New Korea Democratic Party (NKDP) as a memorial message was read by an opposition party official on behalf of party president Lee Min-woo who is now on an overseas trip.

The slogans included, "Get out, NKDP" and "The Kwangju incident should not be utilized for political purposes."

A memorial church service, scheduled for 3 p.m. at YMCA auditorium, was scrapped as it was blocked by police. The prospective participants, instead, held a rally in front of the Kwangju Tourist Hotel about 30 meters away from YMCA, singing hymns and chanting antigovernment slogans.

Demonstrations by about 20 persons and 100 others were staged at two different locations in the afternoon, but they, too, were broken up by police.

300 hold street rally near Myongdong Cathedral

About 300 persons staged street demonstrations near the Myongdong Cathedral after a Mass commemorating the "Kwangju incident" was held Sunday afternoon.

Police whisked away 68 protesters.

The demonstrators were among about 1,000 persons who attended the 4 p.m. Mass at the Cathedral. They began the demonstrations around 8 p.m., but were dispersed by police in about one hour.

35 student activists under probe for roles in rally before YMCA

Police questioned 37 radical youths yesterday who were rounded up for active participation in a demonstration in front of the YMCA building in downtown Seoul ...

... chlight, while Lee Song-il broke the window with a metal bar and shouted antigovernment slogans.

Lee is also reportedly affiliated with Minmintu ...

'87 holidays total 65;

Tentative Plan on Local Auto[redacted]my Due Next Week

The government and the ruling Democratic Justice Party will work out a tentative plan on the implementation of a local autonomy system early next week.

Local self-rule is scheduled to be reintroduced after 25 years during the first half of next year.

The tentative plan, to be adopted at a joint meeting of party and administration officials in charge of studying the system, will be put to public hearings, to be held from next month throughout the nation.

Rep. Koh Kun, chairman of the party's special committee on the study of the local autonomy system, told reporters yesterday, "The government will submit its own plan on the enforcement of the system at the joint meeting."

"We will finalize the tentative plan on the basis of the administration's plan, which contains the party's basic idea," he said.

The party's ideas have been conveyed to the administration through numerous consultations, so far, he said.

However, the tentative plan of the ruling camp will contain "options" on major issues, namely the administrative unit level at which the system should be established first, the method of electing heads of local autonomous bodies, and the number of members of local assemblies, Koh said.

"Through debates on the programs concerned in the public hearings, the final plan will be formulated," he said.

the gathering of the protesters and their storage of demonstration articles. The church has been denying any complication," senior prosecutor Choi

KOREA TIMES

US Embassy Denies Charges of Rape by GIs During Exercise

The U.S. Embassy in Seoul "flatly and categorically" denied allegations by some student groups that there were cases of gang rape by American soldiers committed against two Korean women during the recent "Team Spirit" exercise.

The Embassy said that it had been aware that various versions of a leaflet containing statements extremely critical of the United States had been circulated among some student groups or posted on university campuses.

"The language of that text was so extreme and inflammatory that the Embassy assumed that most people who read it would not take any part of it seriously," the Embassy said in a statement.

It said that the rape charge, however, seemed to have gained credence among some people in Korea.

The Embassy has made inquiries with U.S. military authorities and the Korean police, and has determined that no such incident took place.

"The American Embassy flatly and categorically denies the charges concerning rape in the various versions of the leaflet, and suggests that the same malevolent political motivation reflected in the other parts of that text lay behind the rape charges," the Embassy statement said.

Heilongjiang will open to Soviet ships Tuesday (May 20), the state-run ne agency Xinhua said Monday.

The port is five kilometers (th miles) from the Soviet border and lie the confluence of the Songhua Heilong rivers.

The report said the two countries ducted trade at Tongjiang from 195 the mid-1960s, and the port is be reopened to Soviet vessels to pron Sino-Soviet trade and economic r tions.

The floor leaders of the thre Monday to discuss the holding of s Kim Dong-young of the NDP, Le KNP.

KOREA TIMES

Parties A

The ruling and opposition p agreed yesterday to hold three st committees of the National Ass from Thursday to next Wednes delve into the riot in Inchon on I

The three House panels are Affairs, Education-Information a islation-Judiciary Committees. panel will meet for two days.

The parties also decided to s subcommittee at the Home Affai mittee to investigate the violent strations involving radical stude workers, which foiled the main tion New Korea Democratic Par ly to promote constitutional amer

The accords came in a meeting leaders of the ruling Democratic Party, NDP and the second op Korea National Party.

However, the whips failed to differences on the convocation Steering Committee to handle t tion of forming a special House tee on the constitutional revisi

0039

HANKUK ILBO

漢靑協 발족 4개단체

팀스피리트 美兵士 韓國女人暴行 無根

駐韓대사관 밝혀

◇해방후 나돈 위폐중 가장 정교한것으로 판명된 위폐㊤. 世宗대왕의 얼굴모습이조잡하고 진권㊦보다 바탕의 녹색이 더 짙으며 「경회루」「한국조폐공사제조」등 글자가 없으나 어두운 곳에서는 얼게 식별할수 없을 정도다. 【金泉載전용회선電—傳送 기자】

안양 프리자아파트

쾌적한 주거단지! 획기적인 차

●도심에 위치한 전원 주택단지

●전철역 10분, 각종 편의시설 5분 (시장, 학교, 공공기관, 병원)

●1·2군 구분분양

■ 1차 공급공고

■ 위치 : 안양시 안양동762-2번지외 17필지 ■ 공급규모 : 아파트 15층 6개동 637세대중 3개동 341세대 (기타부대 복리시설) ＊한국화약그룹사원주택조합 42세대 포함.

■ 공급대상 및 공급가격 (단위 : 천원)

형별	군별		공급금액	계약금 (계약시)	1차중도금 ('86.7.19)	2차중도금 ('86.9.19)	3차중도금 ('86.11.19)	4차중도금 ('87.1.19)	잔금 (입주지정일)
76.658㎡ (23.189평)	1군	1 층	22.957	3,257	3,300	3,300	3,300	3,300	6,500
		2.15층 (2.14층)	23.653	3,553	3,400	3,400	3,400	3,400	
	2군	3-14층 (3-13층)	24,348	3,848	3,500	3,500	3,500	3,500	
93.728㎡ (28.353평)	1군	1 층	28.070	5,070	4,000	4,000	4,000	4,000	7,000
		2, 15층	28.920	5,120	4,200	4,200	4,200	4,200	
	2군	3-14 층	29.770	5,170	4,400	4,400	4,400	4,400	

단, 군별란 ( )안 최상층이 14층인 경우 1군 : 1,2,14층. 2군 : 3~13층임.

＊상기공급가에는 각형별 공히 보존등기 등록세가 포함되어 있지 않음. ＊잔금은 은행융자금으로 대체예정 (융자금액은 변경될 수 있음).

■ 입주자 선정

순위	형별(㎡)	신청자격
1순위	공통	○'85.8.19. 이전에 주택청약예금 200만원에 가입하신 분. ○'85.5.19. 이전에 청약저축에 가입하여 '85.5.20. 현재 1순위자로서 '86.5.19.까지 청약예금으로 전환하신 분. ○'80.8.29 이전에 주택은행의 재형저축에 가입하였거나 '81.5.22 이전에 주택청약부금에 가입한 국민주택 청약자격 1순위자로서 '86.5.19 까지 청약예금으로 전환하신 분.
2순위	공통	○주택청약예금 200만원에 가입하여 '86.5.21 현재 3개월 경과하신 분.
3순위	공통	○일반청약자 (주택청약예금과 관계없음). — 청약금 200만원 예치.

＊안양시에 거주하는 세대주 또는 서울특별시 거주자가 주거이전을 목적으로

■ 신청기간 및 장소

순위	신청일자	접수방법및 장소	동호수 추첨및 당첨자발표
1순위	'86.5.20	○접수방법 : 각형별·군별로 접수 1군 : 1,2,15층, 2군 : 3~14층 단, 최상층이 14층인 경우 1군 : 1,2,14층, 2군 : 3~13층 ○접수장소 : 모델하우스	○일시 : '86.5.24 (13:00). ○장소 : 당사 모델하우스 ○추첨 : 신청자및 경찰관 입회하에 당첨자및 동·호수 동시 추첨.
2순위	'86.5.21		
3순위	'86.5.22		

＊선순위자가 공급대상 세대수를 초과할 경우 차순위는 접수치 않음.

＊특별공급 대상자는 '86.5.19 (16:00)까지 당사 모델하우스에 신청.

■ 신청시 구비사항

구분	신청인	구비사항
	공통	○공급신청서 1부, 주택청약예금증서, 주민등록등본 1부
일반공급	본인	○인감및 본인 주민등록증

…격차를 개선하기 위해 합리적 직무와 능력을 중시하는 채용및 고용관행의 확립, 하고 계층간 하후상박에의한 임금조정을 유도한다. 임금체계의 합리화를 위해서는 현행 65~70%인 기본급 비율을 80~90%로 높이고 기본급체계도 속인급·연공급중심에서 직무급·직능급체계로 전환하며 성과에 따른 상여금지급을 결정방법을 권장하는 등 성과배분제도와 연결 운영한다.

▲근로자복지향상=근로자 생활의 지위향상을 위해 주요공단 및 사업체밀집지역에 정부시범사업으로 탁아소(5개소)를 건립, 1세 미만 영아를 가진 여성근로자에 대해서는 무급으로 1년간 휴직할수있는 육아휴직제를 도입…

高麗大生 9백여명 전방入所거부 농성

…시위단순가담자들이기 때문에 후방교육에 보낸 방침이다.

高麗大전방입소교육훈련대상 2학년생 3천4백명중 9백여명은 19일 상오8시30분부터 이날부터 예정된 전방입소교육훈련을 거부하며 교내 중앙도서관을 점거, 철야농성을 벌이고 있다. …이날 하오까지 입소한 학생은 2천4백53명이다.

팀스피리트 기간중 美軍非行說은 모략
美대사관 해명

駐韓美대사관은 최근 여러 전단을 통해 나돌고 있는 팀스피리트훈련기간중 韓國중부지역에서 美軍병사들이 두 韓國人여성을 폭행한 사건이 있었다는 주장에 대해 「美軍당국과 韓國의 경찰당국에 문의한 결과 그러한 사건이 없었다는 단정을 하게 됐다」고 19일 공식부인했다.

…소규모 示威 …에 投石, 파괴

…光州」는 不祥事없이 지나 …

…밤 5·18 …CA에서 열릴 예정이었던 …맞은 18일 추모예배가 경찰의 봉쇄로 …부 대학 무산되자 하오2시40분쯤 숲 …갈전인 시 南NCC회장 尹起石목사 …

0041

U.S. Embassy denies GIs' attack on Korean women during exercise

The U.S. Embassy in Seoul yesterday "flatly and categorically" denied rumors of gang assault committed by American military personnel against two Korean women in the central part of the country during the recent "Team Spirit" exercise.

In the statement, the embassy said it had been aware that various versions of a leaflet containing statements extremely critical of the United States have been circulated among some student groups or posted on university campuses. "The language of that text was so extreme and inflammatory that the embassy assumed that most people who read it would not take any part of it seriously," it said.

One of the charges in the leaflet, however, seems to have gained credence among some people, it said.

The American Embassy has made inquiries with U.S. military authorities and the Korean police, and has determined that no such incident occurred, the statement said.

"The American Embassy flatly and categorically denies the charges concerning rape in the various versions of the leaflet, and suggests that the same malevolent political motivation reflected in the other parts of that text lay behind the rape charges," it said.

0042

MINISTRY OF FOREIGN AFFAIRS
REPUBLIC OF KOREA

Dear Mr. Subbaraman,

I have received your letter of 22 September 1986 together with copies of General Livsey's letter to you and your letter to Mr. Shin, Director General of International Organizations and Treaties Bureau.

From these letters, it is my understanding that you are inquiring about the possibility of using the facilities of the United States Forces in Korea (USFK) by your staff and their family members.

The facilities in question are owned and managed by the USFK and the grant of use of such facilities is to be determined by the USFK in accordance with the provisions of ROK-US Status of Forces Agreement (SOFA).

It is advised, therefore, that you may inquire to the USFK authorities on the matter of using any USFK facilities.

According to the SOFA, however, non-US diplomats are not in the categories of persons authorized to use the USFK facilities.

I hope this information may answer your inquiry.

Sincerely yours,

Tae Kyu Han
Director, Security Division
American Affairs Bureau
Ministry of Foreign Affairs

N.S. Subbaraman
Resident Representative
United Nations
Development Programme

0043

MINISTRY OF FOREIGN AFFAIRS
REPUBLIC OF KOREA

Dear Mr. Subbaraman,

I have received your letter of 22 September 1986 together with copies of General Livsey's letter to you and your letter to Mr. Shin, Director General of International Organizations and Treaties Bureau.

From these letters, it is my understanding that you are inquiring about the possibility of using the facilities of the United States Forces in Korea (USFK) by your staff and their family members.

The facilities in question are owned and managed by the USFK and the grant of use of such facilities is to be determined by the USFK in accordance with the provisions of ROK-US Status of Forces Agreement (SOFA).

It is advised, therefore, that you may inquire to the USFK authorities on the matter of using any USFK facilities.

According to the SOFA, however, non-US diplomats are not in the categories of persons authorized to use the USFK facilities.

I hope this information may answer your inquiry.

국제기구조약국장 : 대

앙고재	안보과	86년 9월 25일	담당	과장	심의관	국장

Sincerely yours,

Tae Kyu Han
Director, Security Division
American Affairs Bureau
Ministry of Foreign Affairs

N.S. Subbaraman
Resident Representative
United Nations
Development Programme

0044

Dear Dr. Hodges,

I would like to call your attention to the advertisement for Englich School by the Korean American Social Associations on which U.S. army officials made a statement denying it as "false".

The statement by U.S. army officials were timely and appropriate to prevent further victims of this kind of fraud.

It will be helpful to us if you let us know whether any U.S. personnel are involved in this business.

Sincerely yours,

Tae Kyu Han

앙 고 재	안보과	86년 5월 19일	담 당	과 장	심의관	국 장

0045

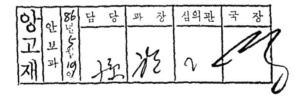

이첩 　　　　　　　　　　　　　　　　　　　일반

법 　　무 　　부

검이 20294- 6200 　503-7052 　1986. 5. 24.

수신 외무부장관 (3년)

참조 미주국장

제목 미8군 한미 문화교류협회 영어강좌 관련 수사상황 통보

1. 미안 20294-19248 (86. 5. 20)과 관련입니다.

2. 미 8군 한미문화교류협회사건에 대하여는 '86.5.15. 동협회 대표 이성희를 사기등 혐의로 구속하여 수사중임을 통보합니다. 끝.

신 경	12395		결재 (공람)		
접수일시	1986. 5. 27				
처리과					

법 무 부 장 관

0046

보내)

내 무 부

형사(지) 23120- 2545 (776-2008) 1986. 6. 10.

수신 외무부장관

참조 미주국장

제목 미 8군 한미 문화교류협회 수사결과 통보

1. 외무부 미안 20294 - 19248 ('86. 5. 20.) 에 관련입니다.

2. 수사결과

가. 피의자 인적사항

주소 : 서울 영등포구 신길 4동 233-11

영어강습소 경영 이 성 희 (39세)

나. 범죄사실

피의자는, '86. 1.초분부터 '86. 5. 14.까지 서울 용산구 한강로 1가 18-2 소재 신생빌딩에 "카사" 라는 무허가 사설영어학원을 운영하면서 허위 과대광고를 하여 이를 믿고 모집에 응한 사람들을 속여 회비명목으로 금품을 편취한 것임.

다. 조 치

피의자를 '86. 5. 15. 서울 용산경찰서에서 학원 및 사설강습소에 관한 법률 위반으로 구속, '86. 5. 23. 검찰에 송치함. 끝.

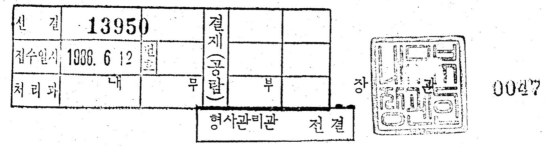

발송 1986. 6. 11 내무부

신 걸	13950	결재(공람)	
접수일시	1986. 6. 12		
처리과			

내 무 부 장 관

형사관리관 전결

0047

공 란

공 란

공　　　란

공 란

공　　　란

공 란

공 란

공　　　란

공 란

공　　　란

공 란

공 란

공 란

공 란

공 란

공　　　란

공 란

공 란

Army agents accused of misconduct

Complaint in ROK includes drug abuse, lost passes

By Neil Roland
United Press International

First of two parts

WASHINGTON — Army counterintelligence authorities in South Korea have condoned widespread misconduct by their special agents, including drug and alcohol abuse, exploitation of agent credentials and private use of government property, a former agent has charged.

Daily alcohol abuse impaired several agents' job performance and led to fistfights with South Koreans, leaving the American soldiers vulnerable to possible blackmail by enemy groups, the former agent said in a written complaint now under investigation by the Army.

JOSEPH DITZHAZY, who filed the 28-page complaint with the Army inspector general's office, also said some intelligence specialists may have allowed a security breach by losing their passes for a top-secret Army facility.

Ditzhazy, who now lives in Arizona, passed a polygraph test about his allegations administered by a former lieutenant colonel who had taught at the Army's intelligence schools.

Other present and former specialists supported Ditzhazy's complaint and agreed that official inaction undercut the effectiveness of Army counterintelligence in South Korea during the past 18 months.

Counterintelligence supervisors responded inadequately when agents complained that colleagues who got into drunken fights sometimes flashed their special credentials to ward off South Korean police, three other intelligence specialists who served in Korea said.

"Very few agents cared," said T.J. Stokes, a former special agent who served in Korea from November 1985 to April 1986. "Command apathy filtered down the ranks. So you had this elite group doing barely enough to get by."

Army counterintelligence agents are assigned to cracking spy and terrorist groups, identifying U.S. security lapses and checking the backgrounds of American soldiers.

The Army's intelligence and security command began informally investigating Ditzhazy's allegations in May and has completed a report that is under review at 8th Army headquarters in Seoul, spokesman Lt. Col. Dick Holk said.

Ditzhazy, who served in South Korea from July 1985 to February 1986, questioned the thoroughness of that investigation, saying no one had yet sought to interview him about his allegations. Stokes, a resident of Georgia, also said she had not been contacted by Army investigators.

Ditzhazy said he sought to report his complaints up the chain of command at the 209th Military Intelligence Company and 524th Military Intelligence Battalion to Sgt. 1st Class Alvin Gloege, 1st Sgt. Luther Moore, Chief Warrant Officer Norman Boring, Capt. Kevin Cunningham and Lt. Col. Charles Narburgh.

DITZHAZY SAID in interviews that he also tried to report complaints to the inspector general of the 501st Group, now a brigade, but Maj. Charles Hawkins avoided him.

Ditzhazy asserted he was harassed in retaliation for his efforts and accused his superiors of unsuccessfully trying to bar his re-enlistment, giving him a very critical written evaluation and twice not recommending him for promotion.

Army spokeswoman Elaine Henrion denied a request for comment from the various supervisors.

The intelligence specialists estimate that eight or nine (of the 20 or so special agents in the Seoul field office) regularly abused alcohol.

The job performance of many agents was impaired by their daily, late-night binges, former agents said.

Intoxicated agents who got into fights with South Korean civilians sometimes displayed their special agent credentials to avoid arrest by South Korean police, intelligence specialists said.

THE SUPERVISORS' failure to address abuses affected bilateral cooperation, Ditzhazy and Stokes said. South Korean agents attached to the Army counterintelligence office distrusted U.S. officials and did not always report problems or share information, they said.

Among examples of official inaction cited:

- No effort was made to report or discipline two intelligence specialists who lost their passes to the Army's top-secret "TANGO" facility while drinking in Seoul.
- Three agents who signed out a government car for professional use during the day were discovered sunbathing at home alongside the vehicle, an intelligence specialist said. A group of agents who sought the car for official purposes reported the incident to Gloege and Boring, but no action was taken, he said.
- An agent regularly made free calls to relatives in the United States on a phone line restricted for official use, Ditzhazy and Stokes said.

Daniloff —— Health ——

[redacted]

0066

공 란

공 란

공 란

공 란

2 PACIFIC STARS AND STRIPES 第3種郵便物認可 **News** WEDNESDAY, SEPTEMBER 24, 1986

USFK rebuts misconduct allegations

By Mike Mooney
Stripes Korea Bureau Chief

SEOUL — Most of the allegations of widespread misconduct by Army counterintelligence agents in South Korea are unsubstantiated, a U.S. Forces Korea spokesman said.

Former Army Sgt. Joseph Ditzhazy made the allegations against members of the 524th Military Intelligence Battalion in South Korea.

Ditzhazy was a member of the 209th Military Intelligence Company prior to his voluntary discharge in April.

USFK public affairs officer Col. Ben Waller said that "Ditzhazy's (allegations) with two exceptions, are not corroborated or supported by the investigation."

Ditzhazy alleged the company and battalion chain of command was unresponsive and unfair and attempted to suppress reports of wrongdoing.

He made the allegations in a 28-page complaint filed with the Army's inspector general's office and also made available to the press.

Ditzhazy alleged that:

● A soldier from Ditzhazy's unit used his Korean National Police identification card to evade arrest by Korean police after a fight in a local bar. Waller said this charge is true.

"A U.S. soldier was involved in an altercation in a bar and did display the KNP card, which was not authorized," he said.

● Investigators did not interview either Ditzhazy or former Sgt. T.J. Stokes in relation to the allegations. Stokes is a former special agent who served in Korea at the same time as Ditzhazy.

Waller said this allegation is also true.

Investigators felt Ditzhazy's 28-page, single-spaced letter spelled out all of his allegations, he said. Waller said investigators did not contact Stokes, since voluntarily discharged due to financial problems, because she was mentioned in the letter only once.

● Daily alcohol abuse impaired several soldiers' job performances.

Waller said interviews with soldiers and members of the chain of command in the 209th MI Co. revealed no proof of widespread alcohol abuse.

● Passes to a top-secret Army facility were lost.

An investigation disclosed no lost or missing passes nor any reports by anyone, including Ditzhazy, of a lost pass to the facility.

● The unit's inspector general, Maj. Charles Hawkins, avoided Ditzhazy.

Waller said Hawkins' records show that Ditzhazy submitted an action request two weeks after arriving in Korea. The request did not list any specific action. Hawkins scheduled or tried to schedule five meetings with Ditzhazy to discuss the request and desired action. Ditzhazy did not keep any of the appointments.

● Wrongdoing on the part of soldiers in the unit was either ignored or covered up.

"He failed to report his suspicions promptly to his chain of command," Waller said. "When the allegations were reported, they were investigated by the proper authority and appropriate action was taken based on the findings."

● Because of alleged abuses, South Korean counterparts did not trust or share information with American colleagues.

Investigators found no evidence of this, Waller said.

● Government vehicles and official telephones were misused by members of the command.

"The investigators found no truth to either charge," Waller said.

● Army Col. Thomas Gray may have revealed secrets after blacking out during a four-day drinking binge with unnamed South Koreans.

"There are, in particular, many inaccuracies and distortions in the allegations concerning Colonel Gray," Waller said.

"It's true that Col. Gray has an alcohol problem. But it's not true that he emerged from a 1985 blackout in the psychiatric ward of the hospital. He voluntarily checked himself into the 121st Evacuation Hospital for alcohol withdrawal and later went to Fort Sam Houston, Texas, where he went through the Army's alcohol rehabilitation program."

Waller called it "regrettable" that Ditzhazy's charges were reported in the news media before completion of the Army investigation, adding that the results of the investigation were being reviewed by 8th Army officials when the story was published.

United Nations

0071

결 번

넘버링 오류

U.S. Embassy denies GIs' attack on Korean women during exercise

The U.S. Embassy in Seoul yesterday "flatly and categorically" denied rumors of gang assault committed by American military personnel against two Korean women in the central part of the country during the recent "Team Spirit" exercise.

In the statement, the embassy said it had been aware that various versions of a leaflet containing statements extremely critical of the United States have been circulated among some student groups or posted on university campuses. "The language of that text was so extreme and inflammatory that the embassy assumed that most people who read it would not take any part of it seriously," it said.

One of the charges in the leaflet, however, seems to have gained credence among some people, it said.

The American Embassy has made inquiries with U.S. military authorities and the Korean police, and has determined that no such incident occurred, the statement said.

"The American Embassy flatly and categorically denies the charges concerning rape in the various versions of the leaflet, and suggests that the same malevolent political motivation reflected in the other parts of that text lay behind the rape charges," it said.

減員인원 축소 罷業 문책않아

美軍·勞組측 합의

임금인상등과 관련, 주한미8군측과 협상을 벌여온 외기노련산하 미8군조합은 11일오전11시 미군측과 △감원대상 7백60명을 2백2명으로 축소하고 △근로자에게 피해를 주는 하청부제는 사전에 적극검토하며 △파업문제와 관련된 일체의 책임을 문지 않는다는 것등 4개항을 합의, 가조인식을 가졌다。

0073

정 리 보 존 문 서 목 록					
기록물종류	일반공문서철	등록번호	32965	등록일자	2009-03-30
분류번호	729.41	국가코드		보존기간	영구
명 칭	SOFA 한.미국 합동위원회 회의 운영 개선, 1988-92				
생 산 과	북미2과	생산년도	1988~1992	담당그룹	
내용목차	1. 1988-89 2. 1992				

0001

1. 1988- 89

0002

공 란

공 란

공 란

공　　　란

공　　　란

공 란

공 란

공 란

공 란

공 란

공 란

공 란

공 란

공 란

공 란

공 란

공 란

공 란

공　　　란

공 란

공 란

공 란

공 란

공 란

공 란

공 란

공 란

공 란

공 란

공 란

공 란

공　　란

공 란

공 란

공 란

공 란

공 란

공　　란

공 란

공 란

2. 1992.

0043

관리 번호	92-187

외 무 부

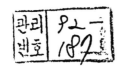

110-760 서울 종로구 세종로 77번지 / (02) 720-2324 / FAX (02) 720-2686

문서번호 미이 01225-847
시행일자 1992. 4. 6.
(경 유)
수 신 수신처 참조
참 조

취급		장 관
보존		
국 장	전 결	
심의관		
과 장		
담 당	조준혁	협조

제 목 한.미 주둔군지위협정(SOFA) 운영 체제 개선

1. 현행 한.미 주둔군지위협정(SOFA) 운영 체제는 1967. 2. 9. 동 협정 발효이후 합동위원회와 13개 분과위원회로 구성되어 현재까지 미군의 한국 주둔에 따르는 제반 사항을 협의, 처리하는 임무를 수행해 왔읍니다.

2. 그러나, 동 SOFA 운영 체제는 그간의 전반적인 한.미 관계의 위상 변화 및 양적인 확대, 주한미군 규모와 역할의 변경등을 감안할 때 그 운영상의 문제점을 개선하고 기능을 활성화시키는 것이 요청되고 있어 당부는 아래와 같이 SOFA 운영 체제 개선 및 활성화 방안을 수립하고 주한미군측과 합의, 시행코자 하는바, 이에 대한 귀부의 동의 여부와 의견을 회보하여 주시기 바랍니다.

예고문에 의거 재분류(1992. 12. 31.)
직위 성명

/계속/

0044

= 아 래 =

가. 현 SOFA 운영상의 문제점

o 각 분과위원회의 경우, 양측 위원장간 직급 (또는 직위)의 차이로 인하여 회의 대리 주재 또는 기피 현상 대두

- 우리측 위원장은 해당부처의 국장급 인사인 반면, 주한미군측은 대부분 대령급 참모

o 따라서 합동위원회의 경우도 위원인 각 분과위원회 위원장의 회의 불참 사례 빈번

- 지난 91. 12월 제170차 합동위원회 회의시 우리측 위원 전원 대리 참석

o 각 분과위원회의 소관 업무도 우리측 해당부처의 경우 그 중요도가 과거에 비해 저하되었거나 일상적(routine) 사안 또는 전문화 됨으로써 국장급의 참여가 불요하게 됨.

- 국장급 위원의 타업무 관련 분주한 일정도 한 원인

나. 개선 및 활성화 방안

o 각 분과위원회의 우리측 위원장의 직급을 현 국장급에서 과장급으로 하향 조정함.

- 각 분과위원회 우리측 간사도 해당과의 SOFA 담당관으로 임명

o 이 경우, 각 분과위원회 우리측 위원장들로 구성된 합동위원회의 우리측 위원의 직급은 자동적으로 하향 조정됨

- 한편 합동위원회 우리측 위원의 숫자도 주한미군측(9명)에 맞춰 적절히 조정

/계속/

0045

o 또한 분과위원회 회의의 효율성 제고를 위해, 관계부처 과장이 전부 참석하는 전체 회의 개최보다 사안에 따라 동 사안의 처리와 직.간접으로 관련된 부처의 해당과장 또는 실무자로 구성된 working - level 소위원회를 개최하여 사안을 협의, 처리

수신처 : 법무부장관(법무실장, 검찰국장, 출입국관리국장), 국방부장관 (정책기획관, 시설국장), 상공부장관(통상진흥국장), 교통부장관 (안전관리국장), 노동부장관(노정국장), 관세청장(심리기획관), 재무부장관(관세국장), 경제기획원장관(물가정책국장), 보건사회부 장관(보건국장), 국립식물검역소장.

0046

2

노 동 부

우 427-760 경기도 과천시 중앙동 1 /전화 (02)504-7338 /FAX 503-9771~2

문서번호 국제 32220-134
시행일자 1992. 4. 13. ( )

수신 외무부장관
참조 미주국장

선결			지시		
접수	일자 시간	92. 4. 15	결재·공람		
	번호	12998			
처리과					
담당자					

제목 한.미 주둔군 지위협정 운영체제 개선 방안에 대한 회신

1. 미이 01225-847 ('92. 4. 7.) 의 관련입니다.

2. 우리부는 귀부의 한.미 주둔군 지위협정 운영 체제 개선방안에 대해 동의함을 회신합니다. 끝.

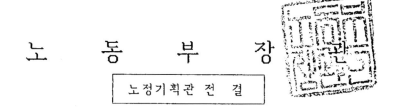

노 동 부 장 관

노정기획관 전 결

0047

조

1/1

관리번호	92-206

관 세 청

우 135-702 서울 강남구 논현동 71 / 전화 (02)512-1123 / 전송 512-0123

문서번호 심리이22760 - 66

시행일자 1992. 4. 15

(경유)

수신 외무부장관

참조 미주국장

선결			지시	
접수	일자 시간	1992. 4. 16 :	결재·공람		
	번호	1450			
처리과					
담당자					

제목 한.미 주둔군 지위협정 (SOFA) 운영체재 개선안 회보

1. 귀 미이 01225 - 847 ('92. 4. 7) 호와 관련입니다.

2. 위호로 문의하신 귀 부의 의견에 동의하며, 아울러 합동위원회 회의시에도 각 분과 위원회 위원장이 전부 참석하는 것 보다는 사안의 처리와 직.간접적으로 관련된 양측 분과 위원회 위원장만이 참석하여 사안을 처리하는 것이 바람직 하다고 생각합니다. 끝.

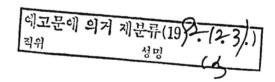

예고문에 의거 재분류(1992.12.31.)
직위 성명

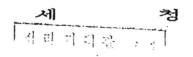

관 세 청

심리기획관

0048

관리번호 92-211

법 무 부

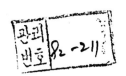

검이 01225- 105 503-7053 1992. 4. 15.

수신 외무부장관

참조 미주국장

제목 한.미주둔군 지위협정(SOFA)운영체제 개선 의견회보

1. 외무부 미이225-847(92.4.7)관련입니다.

2. 귀부에서 추진중인 SOFA 운영체제 개선 및 활성화방안에 대한 의견을 별첨과 같이 회신합니다.

첨부 : SOFA 운영체제 개선 및 활성화방안에 대한 의견1부. 끝.

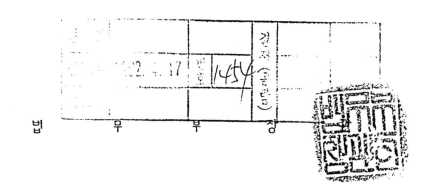

법 무 부 장

0049

SOFA 관계위원회 委員長 職級調整案 檢討

1. 外務部 調整案

o SOFA 관계위원회 各 分科委員長의 職級을 현 局長級에서 課長級으로 하향調整

o 幹事도 해당과 課長級에서 SOFA擔當官으로 任命

2. 調整案 提議背景

o SOFA 관계위원회 各 分科委 兩側委員長間 職級의 差異 (우리측: 주무부처 局長급, 美軍측: 大領급 參謀) 로 인하여 會議代理主宰 또는 不參現象 대두

o 各 分科委 所管業務의 重要度가 과거에 비해 低下되어 局長級의 참여 不要

1

0050

3. SOFA委員會 構成

ㅇ 合同委員會 및 산하 13個 分科委員會로 構成

- 分科委員會 : 시설구역, 형사재판권, 민사청구권, 노무,재무,상무,교통,공공용역,출입국임시,면세물품 불법거래임시,군민관계임시,검역임시, 식물검역임시

ㅇ 合同委員會 構成

- 代表: (韓)외무부 美洲局長, (美)주한미군 副司令官

- 委員: (韓)9개부처局長(檢察局長), (美)주한미군 大領 7名

ㅇ 各 分科委員會 構成

- 代表: (韓)주무부처 局長, (美)주한미군 各 部署大領

- 委員: (韓)9개부처 課長, (美)주한미군 領官級將校

ㅇ 當部 局長이 委員長인 分科委員會

- 刑事재판권 分科委員會 (檢察局長)

- 民事청구권 分科委員會 (法務室長)

- 出入國 임시分科委員會 (出入國 管理局長)

4. 調整案에 대한 檢討意見

肯定的 側面

- o 各 分科委 所管業務가 日常的 事案 또는 專門化됨으로써 局長級 참여 不要
- o 委員會를 관련부처 해당課長 및 實務者로 構成함으로써 기능의 活性化 期待
- o 韓·美間 位相變化등을 고려하여 兩側委員長의 職級을 對等하게 조정함이 相當

否定的 側面

- o 委員長의 職級을 下向調整함으로써, 同委員會의 地位가 全體的으로 格下될 憂慮

檢討 意見

- o 外務部의 調整案대로 개선함이 妥當

조

우 427-760 경기도 과천시 중앙동 1번지/ 전화(02)503-9060/전송 503-9033

문서번호 조정 01255-46

시행일자 '92. 4. 17

(경유)

수신 외무부장관

참조 미주 2과장

선결			결재·공람	
접수	일자 시간	92. 4. 20		
	번호	13658		
처리과				
담당과				

제목 한.미 주둔군지위협정(SOFA) 운영체제 개선

1. 미이 01255-847('92. 4. 7)의 관련입니다.

2. 위 관련 SOFA 운영체제 개선에 대한 귀부(안)에 이견없음을 회신합니다. 끝.

경 제 기 획 원 장

0053

73

상 공 부

427-760 경기 과천시 중앙동 1번지 / 전화(02)503 - 9445 / 전송(02)503 - 9496, 3142

문서번호 통정 01225 -199
시행일자 1992. 4. 18.

수신 외무부장관
참조 미주국장

선결			지시	
접수	일자 시간	92 · 4 · 20	결재·공람	
	번호	13659		
처리과				
담당자				

제목 한.미주둔군 지위협정(SOFA) 운영체제 개선

1. 미이 01225-847('92.4.7) 관련입니다.

2. 대호에 제시된 귀부의 한미주둔군 지위협정(SOFA) 운영체제 개선(안)에 대하여 우리부에서는 이견이 없으며, 상무분과위원장을 다음과 같이 변경함에 동의합니다.

- 다 음 -

현행		개선	
직위	성명	직위	성명
통상진흥국장	장 석 환 (Sokan, Chang)	통상정책과장	신 동 오 (Dongoh, Shin)

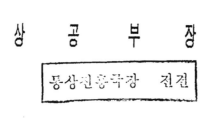

끝.

상 공 부 장

통상진흥국장 전결

0054

2

국 방 부

(792-7671)

연방 24105- 45 1992. 4. 20

수신 외무부장관

참조 미주국장

제목 한.미 주둔군지위협정 운영체제 개선 검토 의견 통보

1. 관련근거 : 미이 01225-847('92.4.7)

2. 귀국의 SOFA 운영체제 개선 및 활성화 방안에 동의하며 이에 따를 경우 당실 SOFA합동위원회 위원은 대미정책담당관(육군대령)이 됨을 통보합니다. 끝.

선 결			결재(공람)		
접수일시	1992. 4. 20	13660			
처리과					

국 방 부 장 관

정책기획관 전결

0055

2

관리번호	92-222

1/1

재 무 부

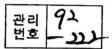

우 427-760 경기도 과천시 중앙동 1 / 전화 5458 / 전송 503-9324

문서번호 관협 22710-88

시행일자 '92. 4 . 22. ( )

수신 외무부장관

참조 미주국장

선결			지시	
접수	일자 시간		결재·공람	
	번호	1580		
처리과				
담당자				

제목 SOFA 운영체제 개선

1. 미이 01225-847 (92.4.7)의 회신입니다.

2. 표제사안과 관련하여 SOFA 각 분과위원회의 위원장의 직급을 하향 조정한다는 귀부의 의견에 동의합니다. 끝.

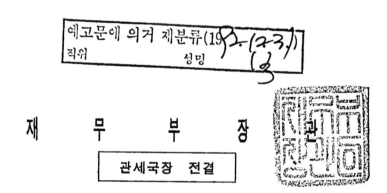

예고문에 의거 재분류(1992.12.31)
직위 성명

재 무 부 장 관

관세국장 전결

0056

2(17)

너와나의 통신보안 국가기밀 보호한다

농 림 수 산 부

우 427-760 경기도 과천시 중앙동 1번지 / 전화(02)503-7255 / 전송(02)503-7249

문서번호 방역 01225-150

시행일자 1992.04.28

수신 외무부장관

			지시		
선결					
접수	일자 시간	92·4·29	결재·공람		
	번호	14913			
처리과					
담당자					

제목 한.미 주둔군 지위협정(SOFA) 운영체제 개선에 대한 회신

1. 미이 01225-847 ('92. 4. 7)호와 관련입니다.

2. 우리부는 귀부의 SOFA 운영체제개선 및 활성화방안에 동의하며, 별도의 의견 없음을 회신합니다. "끝"

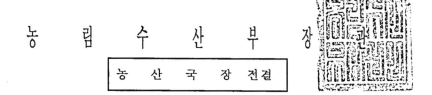

농 림 수 산 부 장

농 산 국 장 전결

0057

21(837)

국 방 부

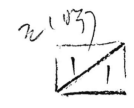

우) 140-023 서울 용산구 용산동3가 1번지 / 전화 (795-6331) / 전송 (796-0369)

문서번호 : 관재 01225-405
시행일자 : 92. 4. 20

수 신 : 외무부장관

참 조 : 미주국장

선결			지시	
접수	일자 시간	14:51	결재 공람	
	번호	1674		
처리과				
담당자				

제 목 : 개선의견 회보

1. 미이 01225-847(92.4.7)의 관련입니다.

2. 한.미 주둔군 지위협정 운영체제 개선방안에 대한 한국측 합동위원회의 의견에 동의하며 그 활성화 방안과 관련해서는 아래사안을 부언하고자 합니다.

가. 분과위원회 회의의 효율성을 위해서 사안에 관련된 실무자 Working Level 소위원회를 통해 처리하는 방안은 효율성에서는 기대되나, 전체회의 개최와 병행해서 운영하는 경우 다소 어려움이 예상됩니다.

나. 따라서,전체회의 개최를 불식하고 소위원회 체제를 정식으로 인정하여 분과위원회 회의에 대체할것인가를 구분해둘 필요가 있습니다. 끝.

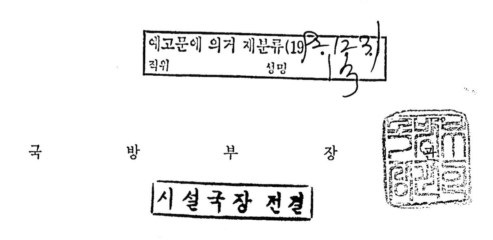

예고문에 의거 재분류(1993.12.31)
직위 성명

국 방 부 장

시설국장 전결

0058

관리번호 92-50P

외 무 부

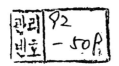

110-760 서울 종로구 세종로 77번지 / (02) 720-2324 / FAX (02) 720-2686

문서번호 미이 01225-
시행일자 1992. 5. 6.
(경 유)
수 신 건 의
참 조

취급		차 관	장 관
보존			
국 장			
심의관		제1차관보	
과 장			
담 당	조준혁		협조

제 목 한.미주둔국지위협정(SOFA) 운영 체제 개선

1. 현행 한.미주둔군지위협정(SOFA : Status of Forces Agreement) 운영 체제는 1967. 2. 9. 동 협정 발효이후 합동위원회와 13개 분과위원회로 구성되어 현재까지 미군의 한국 주둔에 따르는 제반 사항을 협의, 처리하는 임무를 수행해 왔읍니다.

2. 그러나 동 SOFA 운영 체제는 그간의 전반적인 한.미 관계의 위상 변화 및 관련 업무의 양적인 확대, 그리고 주한미군의 규모와 역할의 조정등을 반영하지 못하고 형식에 치우침으로써 현재 하기와 같은 운영상의 문제점들을 노정시키고 있어 그 개선이 요청되고 있는 실정입니다.

- 하 기 -

예고문에 의거 재분류(1992.12.31.)
직위 성명

o 각 분과위원회의 경우, 양측 위원장간 직급(또는 직위)의 차이로 인하여 회의 대리 주재 또는 기피 현상 대두

/계속/

0059

- 우리측 위원장은 해당부처의 국장급 인사인 반면, 주한미군측은 대부분이 대령급 참모

o 따라서 합동위원회의 경우도 위원인 각 분과위원회 위원장의 회의 불참 사례 빈번

- 지난 91. 12월 제170차 합동위원회 회의시 우리측 위원 전원 대리 참석

o 각 분과위원회의 소관 업무도 우리측 해당부처의 경우 그 중요도가 과거에 비해 저하되었거나 일상적(routine) 사안 또는 전문화됨으로써 국장급 인사의 참여가 불요하게 됨

- 국장급 위원의 타업무 관련 분주한 일정도 한 원인

3. 당부는 합동위원회 주관부서로서 그간 현행 SOFA 운영 체제가 상기와 같은 문제점들로 인하여 그 효율성이 극히 저하되었음을 인식, 한.미 안보 협력에 있어서의 주한미군의 중요성을 감안, 이를 시급히 개선하여 그 기능을 활성화하는 것이 바람직하다고 판단, 그 개선 방안을 아래와 같이 수립하고 이를 관계부처와 협의하여 왔는바, 별첨(2)와 같이 관계부처가 이에 동의하여 옴에 따라 이를 주한미군측과 교섭, 합의.시행코자 건의하오니 재가하여 주시기 바랍니다.

- 아 래 -

가. 개선 방안

o 각 분과위원회의 우리측 위원장의 직급을 현 국장급에서 과장급으로 하향 조정함.

- 각 분과위원회 우리측 간사도 해당과의 SOFA 담당관으로 임명

o 이 경우, 각 분과위원회 우리측 위원장들로 구성된 합동위원회의 우리측 위원의 직급은 자동적으로 하향 조정됨.

/계속/

0060

- 한편 합동위원회 우리측 위원의 숫자(12명)도 주한미군측(9명) 에 맞춰 적절히 조정

o 또한 각 분과위원회 회의의 효율성 제고를 위해 관계부처 과장이 전부 참석하는 전체회의 개최보다 사안에 따라 동 사안의 처리와 직.간접으로 관련된 부처의 해당 과장 또는 실무자로 구성된 working-level 소분과위원회를 개최하여 사안을 협의, 처리토록 함.

나. 시행 방안

o 합동위원회 우리측 대표(미주국장) 명의 미측 대표앞 서한(별첨1) 발송

- 현행 SOFA 운영 체제는 1967. 2. 9. 제1차 합동위원회 개최에 즈음하여 교환된 당시 우리측 외무장관과 주한미대사간의 각서에 기초하고 있는바, 동 각서에 의하면 향후 대표단 변경은 합동위원회의 행정사항(administrative function)으로서 합동위원회 양측 대표간에 통보되는 것으로 양해되어 있음.

첨부 : 1. 합동위원회 우리측 대표 명의 미측대표앞 서한(안).
2. 관계부처 동의 공문. 끝.

0061

JOINT COMMITTEE
UNDER
THE REPUBLIC OF KOREA AND THE UNITED STATES
STATUS OF FORCES AGREEMENT

Ronald R. Fogleman
Lieutenant General, USAF
United States Representative

May 8, 1992

Dear General Fogleman,

As you are well aware, the present SOFA system, more specifically the composition of the Joint Committee, is based on the letters exchanged between then Foreign Minister Mr. Il Kwon Chung and then US Ambassador Mr. Winthrop G. Brown back in January, 1967. Since that time, the system has served for the smooth and mutually beneficial solution of the USFK-related matters, and we cannot overestimate its contribution to the ROK-US security cooperation.

However, these days there are growing concerns about the efficiency of the system. And the heart of the concern is that the director-generals in our Government are so much burdened with various kinds of tasks that it is getting harder and harder for them to pay due attention to SOFA-related issues.

Faced with such concerns and in view of the importance of USFK in our bilateral security relationship, I, as ROK representative of the Joint Committee, feel obliged to take necessary measures to reactivate the system. And therefore, I hereby inform you that following persons have been appointed to represent the Government of the Republic of Korea at the Joint Committee and also perform as Charimen of their respective Subcommittees under the provisions of Article XXVIII of the Agreement under Article IV of the Mutual Defense Treaty between the Republic of Korea and the United States of America, regarding the Facilities and Areas and the Status of the United States Armed Forces.

Alternate Representative

Mr. Shin, Il-Soon	Director, the US Policy Division Ministry of National Defense

Deputy Representatives

Mr. Park, Dong-Shik	Director, Public Utility and Price Division Economic Planning Board
Mr. Kang, Suk-In	Director, Customs Cooperation Division Ministry of Finance
Mr. Kim, Jin-Hwan	Director, Second Prosecution Division Ministry of Justice
Mr. Park, Sung-Bok	Director, Residence Control Division Ministry of Justice
Mr. Roh, Yang-Woo	Director, Real Estate Division Ministry of National Defense
Mr. Shin, Dong-Oh	Director, International Trade Policy Division Ministry of Commerce and Industry
Mr. Song, Meng-Yong	Director, International Cooperation Division Ministry of Labor
Mr. Kim, Jin-Youl	Director, Vehicle Policy Division Ministry of Transportation
Mr. Ahn, Chi-Sung	Director, Intelligence Division Korean Customs Administration

Furthermore, I would like to propose that ad-hoc working-level groups be formed under each subcommittee for speedy consultation and resolution of the issues, which will be composed of the members from ministries or agencies relevant with specific issues.

Hoping these changes will greatly enhance the efficiency of the SOFA system, I remain,

Sincerely yours,

Chung Yae Ik
Director-General
American Affairs Bureau, MOFA
ROK Representative

JOINT COMMITTEE
UNDER
THE REPUBLIC OF KOREA AND THE UNITED STATES
STATUS OF FORCES AGREEMENT

15 May 1992

Mr. CHUNG Tae Ik
Director General
American Affairs Bureau
Ministry of Foreign Affairs
Republic of Korea Representative

Dear Director General CHUNG:

I was very pleased to receive your letter regarding a restructuring of the ROK component to the Joint Committee. I agree with your analysis and strongly support actions that facilitate smooth and efficient operations to resolve bilateral issues under the US-ROK SOFA.

Your proposal to allow subcommittees to form tailored working-groups designed especially to deal with specific issues is long overdue and demonstrates sincere desire to further smooth operations of the SOFA Joint Committee system.

I, too, hope that the work we due as our national representatives to the Joint Committee continues to enhance the efficiency and credibility of the Joint Committee while strengthening the already strong ties of the US-ROK Security relationship.

Ronald R. Fogleman
Lieutenant General
United States Air Force
United States Representative

0065

외 무 부

110-760 서울 종로구 세종로 77번지 / (02) 720-2324 / FAX (02) 720-2686

문서번호 미이 01225-847
시행일자 1992. 5. 19.
(경 유)
수 신 수신처 참조
참 조

취급		장 관
보존		(서명)
국 장	전 결	
심의관	(서명)	
과 장	(서명)	
담 당	조준혁	협조

제 목 한.미 주둔군 지위협정(SOFA) 운영 체제 개선

연 : 미이 01225-847

1. 표제 관련, 연호 당부(안)에 대해 주한미군측이 92. 5. 15자로 동의하여 옴에 따라 SOFA 운영 체제가 동일자로 아래와 같이 변경.시행됨을 알려드립니다.

- 아 래 -

가. 합동위원회

o 대 표 : 외무부 미주국장

o 교체대표 : 외무부 미주국 심의관

o 위 원 : 경제기획원 조정과장
재 무 부 관세협력과장
법 무 부 검찰2과장
법 무 부 송무과장

/계속/

0066

국 방 부 대미정책과장

국 방 부 관재과장

상 공 부 동상정책과장

노 동 부 국제협력과장

교 통 부 차량과장

o 간 사 : 외 무 부 북미2과장

나. 분과위원회

o 8개 정규 분과위원회

- 위원장 : 상기 합동위원회 해당 위원

- 간 사 : 해당위원 소속과 SOFA 담당관

o 임시 분과위원회 위원장 및 간사

- 출입국 임시 : 법무부 체류심사과장

- 면세물품 불법거래 임시 : 관세청 정보과장

- 군민관계 임시 : 외무부 북미2과장

- 방역 임시 : 보건사회부 방역과장

- 식물검역 임시 : 농림수산부 식물방역과장

(간사는 각 위원장 소속과의 SOFA 담당관)

다. Working-level 소분과위원회 운영

- 각 분과위원회 회의의 효율성 제고를 위해 관계부처 과장들이 전부 참석하는 분과위원회 전체 회의 개최보다 사안에 따라 동 사안의 처리와 직.간접으로 관련된 부처의 해당과장 또는 실무자로 구성된 working-level 소분과위원회를 개최하여 사안을 협의.처리함.

/계속/

0067

2. 아울러 현재 당부는 SOFA 합동위원회 제171차 회의를 6. 26.경 개최할 것을 준비중에 있음을 통보하니 업무에 참고하시기 바랍니다.

수신처 : 경제기획원장관(물가정책국장), 재무부장관(관세국장), 법무부장관 (법무실장, 검찰국장, 출입국관리국장), 국방부장관(정책기획관, 시설국장), 상공부장관(통상진흥국장), 노동부장관(노정국장), 교통부장관(안전관리국장), 관세청장(심리기획관), 보건사회부장관 (보건국장), 농림수산부장관(농산국장).

0068

외 무 부

110-760 서울 종로구 세종로 77번지 / (02) 720-2324 / FAX (02) 720-2686

문서번호 미이 01225- 68
시행일자 1992. 6. 10.
(경 유)
수 신 수신처 참조
참 조

취급		장 관
보존		
국 장	전 결	
심의관	출장中	
과 장		
담 당	조준혁	협조

제 목 SOFA 운영 활성화

연 : 미이 01225-847, 54

1. 당부는 그간 SOFA 운영 체제가 각 분과위원회 위원장(합동위원회 위원) 상호간 직급의 차이 및 회의 운영에 있어서의 형식 위주등으로 인하여 그 효율성에 있어서 문제가 있어 왔음을 감안, 연호와 같이 SOFA 운영 체제를 전반적으로 개선한 바 있읍니다.

2. 이와 관련, SOFA 운영을 보다 활성화하기 위하여는 상기 체제 개편을 계기로 각 분과위원회별로 주한미군측 해당 분과위원회 위원 명단 파악, 위원장 및 간사 상호간 정기 또는 수시 접촉, 분과위 소관 업무의 파악 등이 필요하다고 사료됩니다.

/계속/

0069

3. 당부로서도 SOFA 관련 업무의 원활한 처리를 위하여 합동위원회 또는 여타의 기회를 통하여 우리측과 주한미군측 상호간의 이해 증진과 유대 강화를 위하여 노력할 것인 바, 귀부(처) 소관 분과위원회를 운영함에 있어 문제점이 있으면 당부로 통보하여 주시기 바랍니다. 끝.

수신처 : 경제기획원장관(물가정책국장), 재무부장관(관세국장), 법무부장관(법무실장, 검찰국장, 출입국관리국장), 국방부장관(정책기획관, 시설국장), 상공부장관(통상진흥국장), 노동부장관(노정기획관), 교통부장관(안전관리국장), 관세청장(심리기획관), 보건사회부장관(보건국장), 농림수산부장관(농산국장).

0070

분과위원회 설치 경위

[8개 분과위 + 3개 임시분과위]

1. 8개 분과위(67.1.16 및 1.19 예비 실무자회의)

   o 아측, 분과위 설치와 관련 하기 제의
     - 7개 분과위(시설구역, 형사, 민사, 노무, 재무, 상무, 교통)
       설치 제의
     - 출입국, 보건위생, 예비역훈련 관련사항 처리위해 임시분과위
       설치 가능

   o 미측, 7개 분과위 및 출입국 임시분과위 설치에 동의
     - 보건위생 임시분과위 설치는 부여할 과제 발생시 까지 연기할 것을
       제의

   o 아측, 미측 제의에 동의

2. 공공용역 분과위

   o 15차 합동위(67.9.28), 상무 분과위에 SOFA 6조(공익사업과 용역)
     관련사항 협의절차에 관한 과제 부여

   o 상무 분과위, 합동위에 하기 건의 상정
     - 상무 분과위는 SOFA 6조 관련사항에 대해서 임무 해제
     - 동 사항을 담당할 공공용역 분과위 신설

   o 20차 합동위(68.1.18), 상무 분과위 건의 승인

0071

3. 군민관계 임시 분과위

- 71.9.2 합동위 대표간 긴급조치로써 군민관계 임시분과위 설치

  (임 무)

  - 주한미군 및 미군부대 종사 또는 인근지역 거주 한국인이 관련된 문제 조사, 분석
  - 한.미 관계에 부정적 영향을 미칠 조건을 제거하고 미군과 한국인간 상호 이해 및 조화관계 증진을 위해 필요한 예방조치를 건의

4. 면세물품 임시분과위

- 74.4.24 합동위 미측대표, 면세물품 불법거래 방지 위해 긴급조치로써 임시분과위 설치 제의

- 74.5.1 합동위 아측대표, 미측제의에 동의

- 74.5.6 합동위 대표간 긴급조치로써 면세물품 임시분과위 설치

0072

US-ROK JOINT COMMITTEE - ROK COMPONENT

ROK REPRESENTATIVE		**Telephone**
Mr. Ki-Moon Ban	Director General American Affairs Bureau Ministry of Foreign Affairs	720-2320
ALTERNATE REPRESENTATIVE		
Mr. Soung-Jin Chung	Assistant Minister Office of Legal Affairs Ministry of Justice	503-7006
DEPUTY REPRESENTATIVE		
Mr. Kun-Ho Cho	Director General Customs & Tariff Bureau Ministry of Finance	503-9291
Mr. Myung-Boo Choi	Assistant Minister Prosecution Ministry of Justice	503-7007
Mr. Shi-Pyung Kim	Director General Immigration Bureau Ministry of Justice	503-7010
Mr. Seong-Tae Cho	Director Office of Policy & Plan Ministry of National Defense	795-0071
Mr. Hae-Jong Lee	Director General Installation Bureau Ministry of National Defense	795-0071

0073

Mr. Sokan Chang	Director General International Trade Promotion Bureau Ministry of Trade & Industry	503-9442
Mr. Chang-Won Kim	Director General Safety Management Bureau Ministry of Transportation	392-8025
Mr. Sang-Nam Kim	Director General Labour Policy Bureau Ministry of Labour	504-7338 - 9
Mr. Chang-Lae Park	Director General Investigation Bureau Korean Customs Administration	512-2005

SECERETARY

Mr. Ho-Jin Lee	Director North America Divison II Ministry of Foreign Affairs	720-2239,2324

ASSISTANT SECRETARY

Mr. Jai-Hyon Yoo	Deputy Director North America Divison II Ministry of Foreign Affairs	"
Mr. Byung-Jae Cho	Assistant Director North Amercia Divison II Ministry of Foreign Affairs	"
Mr. June-Hyuck Cho	"	"
Mr. Jin Hur	"	"
Mr. Chong-Suk Choi	"	"

0074

정 리 보 존 문 서 목 록					
기록물종류	일반공문서철	등록번호	2012090605	등록일자	2012-09-19
분류번호	729.41	국가코드		보존기간	영구
명 칭	SOFA 한.미국 합동위원회, 제169차, 1991.6.7				
생 산 과	안보정책과	생산년도	1990~1991	담당그룹	
내용목차	* 1990.7.27. 예정이었으나 SOFA 개정교섭으로 연기 개최				

0001

공 란

공 란

공 란

강안

건 설 부

수도 30343-7282 (503-7377) 1990. 3. 30
수신 외무부장관 (준영구)
참조 미주국장
제목 공공용역분과위원 변경 통보

'90. 3. 26 대통령령 제12.959호에 의거 우리부 직제가 개편됨에 따라 공공용역분과위원이 다음과 같이 변경되었기 통보합니다.

다 음

당 초	변 경	비 고
상하수도국 수도계획과장 정 덕 규	상하수도국 수도정책과장 박 의 환	

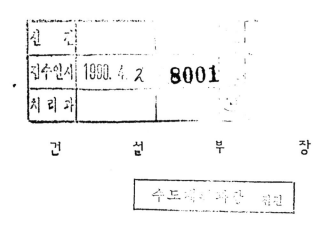

끝.

신 간		
접수일시	1990. 4. 2	8001
처리과		

건 설 부 장

수도정책과장 전결

0005

공 란

공 란

공 란

공 란

공 란

공 란

공　　란

공 란

공 란

공 란

공 란

공 란

공 란

공 란

공 란

공 란

공 란

공 란

공 란

공 란

공　　　란

MINISTRY OF FOREIGN AFFAIRS
REPUBLIC OF KOREA

16 April, 1990

Dear Dr. Hodges:

I would like to acknowledge receipt of your letter dated April 9, 1990, in which you proposed to record in the minutes of the next SOFA Joint Committee Meeting the "Memorandum of Agreement Between the United States Forces, Korea and the Republic of Korea, Ministry of National Defense, Reference Theater Communications Cost Sharing."

It is the view of the ROK side of the Joint Committee that the said MOA was concluded outside the Joint Committee channels and its contents have little relevance with the SOFA. Therefore, we deem it unnecessary to present the MOA in the Joint Committee and to record the MOA in the Joint Committee minutes.

Sincerely

SONG MIN SOON
ROK Secretary
ROK-US Joint Committee

Dr. Carroll B. Hodges
US Secretary
ROK-US Joint Committee

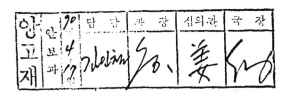

안고재	안보과	90 4 17	담 당	과 장	심의관	국 장
			[signature]	[signature]	姜	[signature]

0027

산업통상 사무회의 경제단국 이거대자

깅인(결)

경 제 기 획 원

조정 10311- 136 (503-9060) '90. 4. 23.

수신 외무부장관

제목 주한 미군 적용 사유화차 운송취급 규칙(철도청고시)개정 수락 통보

1. (당원) 조정 10311 - 378('89.12.15)호와 관련입니다.

2. 위와 관련하여 당원이 미측에 제의한 주한 미군 적용 사유화차 운송취급 규칙(철도청 고시) 개정에 대하여 미측에서는 별첨 사본과 같이 제안내용에 동의할 것을 당원에 통보하여 온바, 이를 차기 SOFA 합동위에 상정될수 있도록 조치하여 주시기 바랍니다.

첨부 : 1. 미측 공공용역 분과위원회 공문 사본 1부.
2. SOFA 합동위원회 상정 안건 1부. 끝.

발송 1990. 4. 23 경제기획원

경 제 기 획 원 장

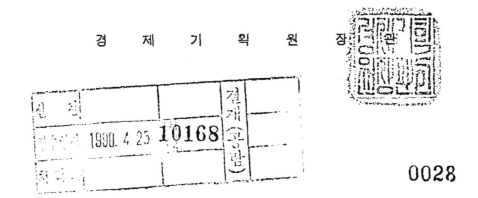

신 전			결재(공람)
접수일시 1990. 4. 25	10168		
처 리 과			

0028

공　　　　란

공 란

공 란

공 란

공 란

가이

대 한 민 국

상 공 부

통 정 20294- 631 503-9445 1990.5.1.

수 신 외무부장관

참 조 미주국장

제 목 SOFA 합동위 상무분과위원회 명단 통보

SOFA 합동위원회 상무분과위원회 한국측 명단을 별첨과 같이 통보하니"위원회 및 분과위원회 관계관 명단" 변경등 귀업무에 참고하여 주시기 바랍니다.

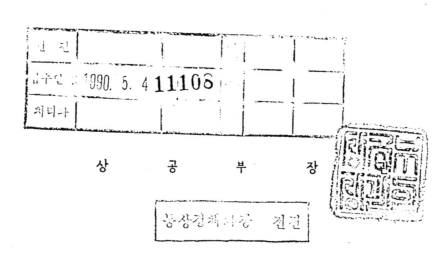

첨 부 : 명단1부. 끝.

1990. 5. 01

선 결				
접수일시 1990. 5. 4	11106			
처리과				

상 공 부 장

통상진흥국장 전결

0034

상무분과 위원회 - 한국측

위 원 장

이 순 우	상공부 통상진흥국장	503 - 9442

교체 위원장

이 기 성	상공부 통상협력관	503 - 9443

간 사

신 동 오	상공부 통상정책과장	503 - 9444

부 간 사

유 종 순	상공부 통상진흥국 통상정책과	503 - 9445

위 원

김 기 수	내무부 치안본부 외사부장	313 - 0848
이 영 회	재무부 세제국 국제조세과장	503 - 9288
구 창 덕	법무부 출입국관리국 입국심사과장	503 - 7095
김 종 희	상공부 상역국 무역정책과장	503 - 9432
정 기 수	상공부 상역국 수입과장	503 - 9440
김 원 배	노동부 노정국 노정과장	503 - 9730
권 희 석	외무부 미주국 안보과	720 - 2324

0035

COMMERCE SUBCOMMITTEE-ROK COMPONENT

CHAIRMAN		TELEPHONE EXCHANGE
Mr. Lee Soon Woo	Director-General, Int'l Trade Promotion Bureau Ministry of Trade and Industry	503 - 9442

ALTERNATE CHAIRMAN

Mr. Lee Ki Sung	Director-General Trade Cooperation Bureau Ministry of Trade and Industry	503 - 9443

SECRETARY

Mr. Shin Dong Oh	Director, Int'l Trade Policy Division Int'l Trade Promotion Bureau Ministry of Trade and Industry	503 - 9444

ASSISTANT SECRETARY

Mr. Yoo Chong Soon	Deputy Director Int'l Trade Policy Division Int'l Trade Promotion Bureau Ministry of Trade and Industry	503 - 9445

MEMBERS

Mr. Kim Ki Soo	Superintendent General, Foreign Affairs Bureau Korean National Police Headquarters Ministry of Home Affairs	313 - 0848

0036

Mr. Lee Young Hoi	Director, International Tax Division Tax Bureau Ministry of Finance	503 - 9288
Mr. Koo Chang Deok	Director, Entry Control Division Bureau of Immigration Ministry of Justice	503 - 7095
Mr. Kim Jong Hee	Director, Trade Policy Division Trade Bureau Ministry of Trade and Industry	503 - 9432
Mr. Chung Kee Soo	Director, Import Division Trade Bureau Ministry of Trade and Industry	503 - 9440
Mr. Kim Won Bae	Director, Labor Policy Division Bureau of Labor Policy Ministry of Labor	503 - 9730
Mr. Kwon Hee Seog	National Security Division American Affairs Bureau Ministry of Foreign Affairs	720 - 2324

0037

무심코 던진말이 국가기밀 누설한다

가인

농 림 수 산 부

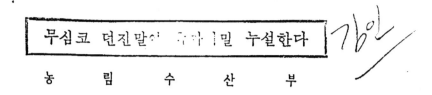

방역 27151-323 503-7255 1990. 5. 7.

수신 외무부장관

참조 안보과장

제목 SOFA 합동위 산하 식물검역 임시분과위 위원 명단 변경

1. 관련 : 미안 01225- 10591 ('90. 3. 12).

2. SOFA 합동위 산하 식물검역 임시분과위원회의 한국측 위원 명단을 별첨과 같이 변경하였기 통보합니다.

첨부 : SOFA 식물검역 임시분과위 명단 (국, 영문) 1부. 끝.

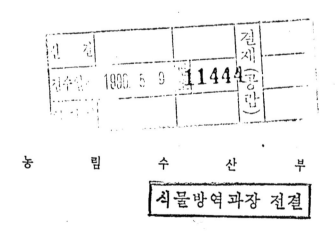

발송
1990. 5. 07
농림수산부

선결			결재(공람)
접수일시 1990. 5. 9	11444		

농 림 수 산 부 장 관

식물방역과장 전결

0038

SOFA 식물검역 임시분과위원회 (한국측) 명단

		전화번호
위원장		
안 선 환	국립식물검역소장	(0343)49-0523
교체위원장		
홍 인 식	농림수산부 식물방역과장	503-7255
간 사		
심 성 섭	국립식물검역소 국제검역정보과장	(0343)45-1223
위 원		
김 광 웅	농림수산부 식물방역과 검역주무	503-7255
박 창 용	국립식물검역소 국제검역정보과 제1계주무	(0343)46-1926
신 현 포	" 조사연구과 이화학주무	(0343)45-1225
공 효 상	" 검역과 기획주무	(0343)49-0524
김 진 성	" 국제검역정보과	(0343)46-1926
진 용 태	" 인천지소장	(032)72-1540
조 병 재	외무부 안보과	720-2324

0039

AD HOC SUBCOMMITTEE ON PLANT QUARANTINE

(ROK COMPONENT)

Chairman		Telephone Exchange
Mr, AHAN Sin Hwan	Director General National Plant Quarantine Service	(0343)49-0523
Alternate Chairman		
Mr. HONG In Shik	Director Plant Protection Div., MAFF	503-7255
Secretary		
Mr. SHIM Seong Seop	Director Int'l. Quarantine Information Div. , NPQS	(0343)45-1223
Members		
Mr. KIM Kwang Woong	Assistant Director Plant Protection Div., MAFF	503-7255
Mr. PARK Chang Yong	Assistant Director Int'l.Quarantine Information Div.,NPQS	(0343)46-1926
Mr.SHIN Hyun Po	Assistant Director Investigation & Research Div., NPQS	(0343)45-1225
Mr. Kong Hyo Sang	Assistant Director Quarantine Div.,NPQS	(0343)49-0524
Mr.KIM Jin Seong	Plant Quarantine Officer Int'l .Quarantine Information Div.,NPQS	(0343)46-1926
Mr. JIN Yong Tae	Director Incheon Branch, NPQS	(032) 72-1540
Mr. CHO Byoung Jae	National Security Division American Affairs Bureau Ministry of Foreign Affairs	720-2324

0040

국 방 부

관재 01237-558 795-6331 1990. 5. 14

수신 외무부장관

참조 미주국장

제목 과제상정

1. 당부는 동두천시로부터 신천 개수공사와 관련한 주한미군 전용훈련장 (7 X - 27)부지 일부 약 2.19 에이카에 대한 사용협의 요청을 접하였습니다.

2. 상기 요청토지의 해제반환에 따른 한미간 계속적인 협의를 위해 S.O.F.A 합동위원회에 과제상정 하오니 이를 시설구역분과 위원회의 과제로 위촉하여 주시기 바랍니다. 끝.

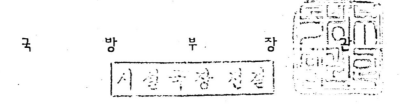

발송 1990. 5. 14 국방부

국 방 부 장 관

시설국장 전결

12007

0041

예고: 재분류

건 설 부

수관 30343 - 1228 503 -7337 1990. 5. 22.

수신 외무부 장관

참조 미주국장

제목 공공용역 분과 위원변경 통보

'90. 3. 26. 대통령령 제12959호에 의거 우리부 직제가 개편됨에 따라 공공용역 분과위원이 다음과 같이 변경되었기 통보합니다.

- 다 음 -

당 초	변 경	비 고
상하수도국 수도정책과장 박 의 환	상하수도국 수도관리과 이 두 헌	90. 3. 28.

끝.

건 설 부 장 관

수도관리과장 전결

13108

0042

가인

국 방 부

관재 01237-670 795-6331 '90. 6. 2

수신 외무부장관

참조 미주국장

제목 과제상정

1. 당부는 침국군으로부터 왜관 공단이주단지 건설공사와 관련한 주한미군 송유관 (MP.71.5)의 이설협의 요청을 접하였습니다

2. 상기건의 한미간 계속적인 협의를 위하여 S.O.F.A 합동위원회에 과제상정 하오니 이를 시설구역분과위원회의 과제로 위촉하여 주시기 바랍니다. 끝.

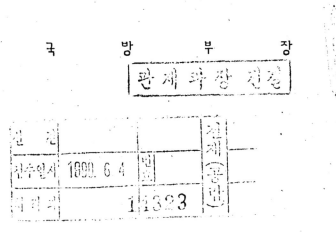

발송승
1990. 6. 02
국방부

국 방 부 장 관

관재과장 전결

선 결			결재 (공란)
접수일시	1990. 6. 4	번호	
처리과	11323		

0043

가인 (담당)

국 방 부

관재 01237-684 795-6331 '90. 6. 7.

수신 외무부장관
참조 미주국장
제목 과제상정

1. 우리부는 철도건설창으로부터 과천선 복선 전철공사에 저촉이 되는 주한미군 송유관 2개소(MP. 245.3, 247)에 대한 보호 협의 요청을 접하였습니다

2. 상기건의 한미간 원만한 해결을 위하여 SOFA 합동위원회에 과제상정 하오니 이를 시설구역분과위원회의 과제로 위촉하여 주시기 바랍니다. 끝.

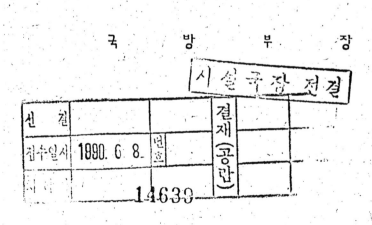

발송 1990. 6. 07 국방부

국 방 부 장

국방부장관인

시설구장 전결

선 결			결재(공람)	
접수일시	1990. 6. 8.	번호		
처리과	14639			

0044

교 통 부

차량 33150 - 741 (392 - 9707) '90. 7. 16.

수신 수신처 참조

제목 SOFA 교통분과위원회 위원경질 통보

SOFA 교통분과위원회 한국측 위원(교통부)이 별첨과 같이 경질되었기 통보합니다.

첨부 SOFA 교통분과위원회 명단(한국측) 1부. 끝.

선 결			결재(공람)	
접수일시	1990. 7. 16	번호		
처리과		19398		

교 통 부 장 관

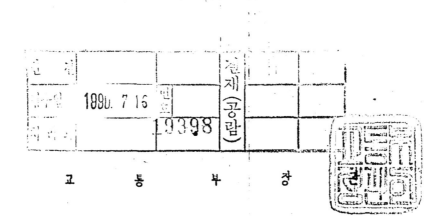

수신처 외무부(미국안보과), 교통분과위원회 미측간사(Maj Malcolm H. Perkins)

0045

SOFA 교통분과위원회 명단(한국측)

구 분	소 속	직 위	성 명	비고
위원장	교통부	안전관리국장	김경회 (KIM KYUNG HOI)	신임
교체위원장	"	항공국장	이헌석 (LEE HEON SEOK)	신임
간사	"	안전관리국 차량과장	김진열 (KIM JIN YOUL)	
위원	내무부 치안본부	교통지도과장	이재열 (LEE JAE YOUL)	
	교통부	수송정책국 해운정책과장	박영삼 (PARK YOUNG SAM)	신임
	"	수로국 측량과장	김성식 (KIM SUNG SIK)	
	"	서울지방항공관리국 관리과장	이환건 (LEE HWAN GUAN)	
	철도청	운수국화물과장	이율재 (LEE YUL GAI)	
	공군본부	군수참모부 수송처장	이윤수 (YI YUN SU)	
	해군본부	"	김문선 (KIM MOON SUN)	
	육군본부	군수참모부		

0046

공 란

공 란

공 란

공 란

공 란

국 방 부

관재 01237-1010 795-6331 '90. 8. 16.

수신 외무부장관

참조 미주국장

제목 과제 상정

1. 우리부는 서울지방국토관리청으로부터 IBRD 6차 도로차관사업 41 공구인 첨부도면 표시지역 수원 - 인덕원간 소재 주한미군 송유관 (MP 238-243)의 이설협의 요청을 접하였습니다.

2. 상기건의 한미간 계속적인 협의를 위해 SOFA 합동위원회에 과제상정 하오니 이를 시설구역분과위원회 과제로 위촉하여 주시기 바랍니다.

첨부 : 위치도 1부 끝.

발송 1990. 8. 16 국방부

국 방 부 장

관재과장 전결

분 전			결재 (공람)	
접수일시	1990. 8. 17			
처리과	22795			

5

0052

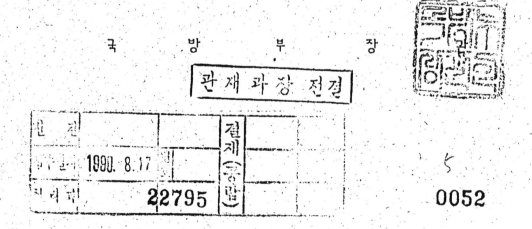

1.位置図

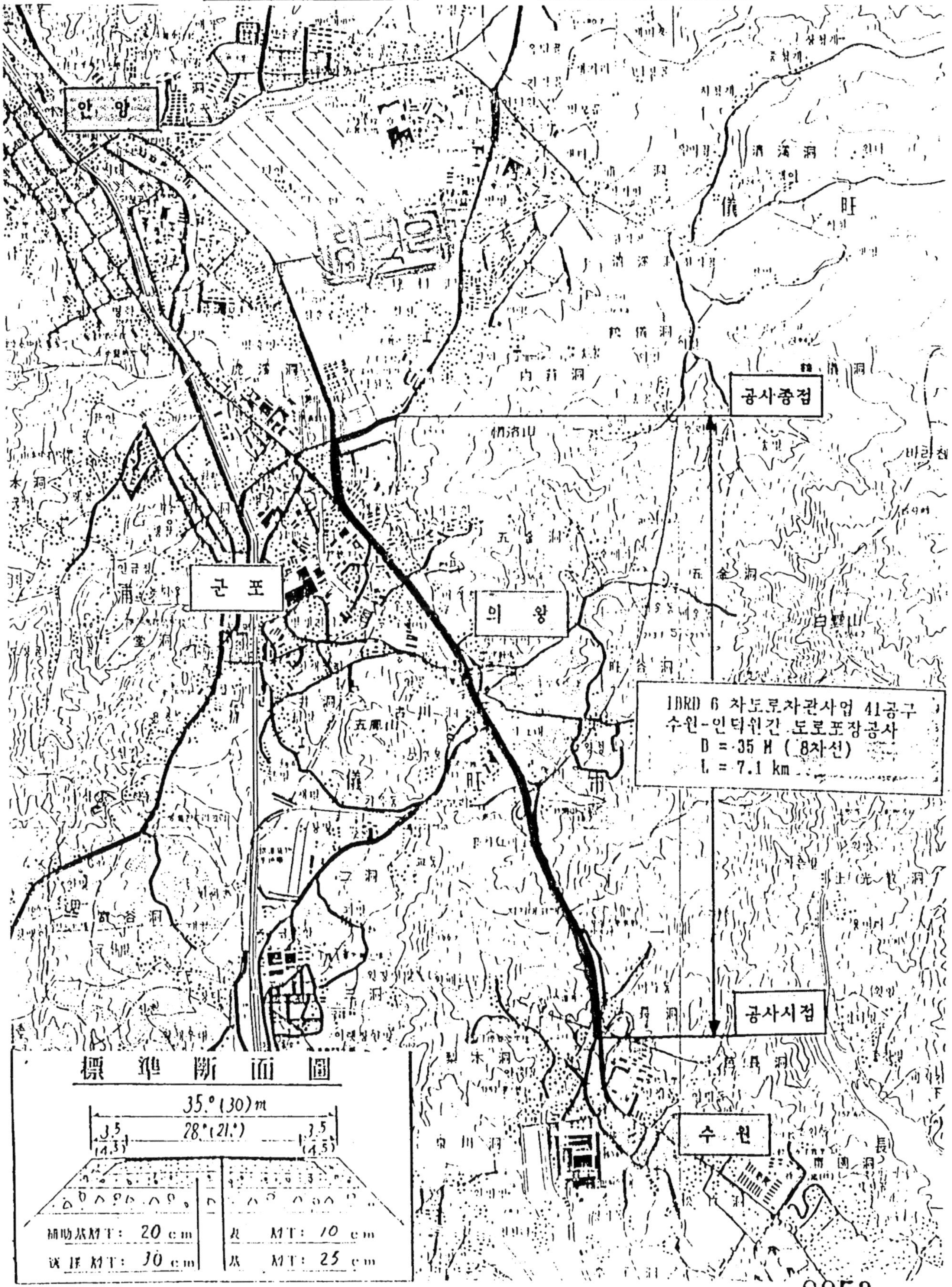

안 양
군 포
의 왕
수 원
공사종점
공사시점
IBRD 6 차도로차관사업 41공구
수원-인덕원간 도로포장공사
D = 35 M (8차선)
L = 7.1 km
標 準 斷 面 圖
35.0 (30) m
28.0 (21.0)
3.5 (4.5)
3.5 (4.5)
20 cm
30 cm
10 cm
25 cm

0053

가인

국 방 부

관재 01237 - 1141 795 - 6331 90. 9. 12.

수신 외무부 장관 (미주국장)

제목 과제상정

1. 동두천시는 동시 보산동 소방도로 개설공사에 편입되는 주한미군사 시설(캠프 케이시) 약 0.006에이카를 해제반환 요청하고 있읍니다.

2. 본건의 한·미간 계속적인 협의를 위하여 SOFA 합동위원회에 과제상정하오니 시설구역 분과위원회 과제로 위촉하여 주시기 바랍니다.

발송승
1990. 9. 12
국방부

25728

국 방 부 장 관

0054

국 방 부 기안

관재 01237- 1192 795-6331 90. 9. 24.

수신 외무부장관

참조 미주국장

제목 과제 상정

1. 우리부는 충남 천안시 및 경북 경주군에 소재하는 주한미군송유관에 대산 보호협의 요청을 받고, 이를 주한미군과 협의하기 위하여 아래와 같이 SOFA 합동위원회에 과제상정하오니 시설구역 분과위원회의 과제로 위촉하여 주시기 바랍니다.

가. 과제 1

1) 요청기관 : 천안시

2) 내 용 : 천안시 동부간선도로 개설공사 구간내에 있는 송유관 보호 (MP 194.5)

나. 과제 2

[redacted]

2) 내 용 : 경주군 안강읍 두류리 소재의 요청인 소유주유소 진입로 개설을 위한 송유관 보호 (MP 17.5). 끝.

1990. 9. 26
국방부

국 방 부 장 관

27191

0055

국 방 부

관재 01237- 1214 795-6331 90. 9. 28.

수신 외무부장관

참조 미주국장

제목 과제상정 의뢰

1. 우리부 예하 공군은 예천기지내의 주한미군 비상용물자 저장부지를 이전하기 위하여 동부지를 해제반환 받고자 합니다.

2. 본건의 한.미간 계속적인 협의를 위하여 SOFA합동위원회에 과제 상정하오니 시설구역분과위원회 과제로 위촉하여 주시기 바랍니다. 끝.

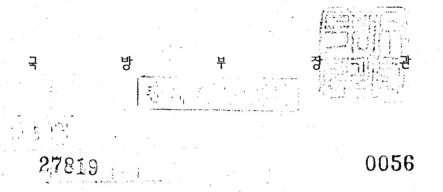

발신 1990. 9. 29. 국방부

국 방 부 장 관

27819

0056

공 란

공 란

가인

경 제 기 획 원

조정 10311-385 (503-9060) 문서담당 이무관 '90. 10. 13.
수신 외무부장관
제목 주한미군 적용 전력요금 개정 수락 통보

1. (당원) 조정 10311 - 381('90.10.10)호와 관련입니다.

2. 위와 관련하여 당원이 미측에 제의한 주한미군 적용 전력요금 개정 문제에 대하여, 미측에서는 별첨사본과 같이 제안내용에 동의하여 온 바, 귀부에서는 이를 차기 SOFA합동위에서 협의될 수 있도록 조치 바랍니다.

첨부 1. 미측 공공용역분과위원회 공문사본 1부.
2. SOFA합동위원회 협의 안건 1부. 끝.

발송 1990.10.13 경제기획원

경 제 기 획 원 장 관

물가정책국장 전결

0059

28826

공 란

공 란

공 란

공　　　　란

법 무 부

송심 01600-14658 503-7041 1990. 11. 8.

수신 외무부 장관

참조 미주국장

제목 SOFA 합동위원회 산하 분과위원회 위원변경통보

1. 법무부 송심01600-14450(90.11.3)호와 관련입니다.

2. 법무부직제개정에 따라 주둔군 지위협정(S.O.F.A)합동위원회 산하 민사청구권분과위원회및 시설구역분과위원회 위원이 다음과 같이 변경되어 통보하오니 업무에 참고하시기 바랍니다.

" 다 음 "

위원회명	직책	변경 사항	
		변 경 전	변 경 후
민사청구권 분과위원회	간사	법무부 법무실 송무과장 안승군	법무부 법무실 송무담당관 신광옥
	위원	" " 법무과장 신광옥	" " 법무과장 명노승
시설구역분과 위 원 회	위원	" " 송무과장 안승군	" " 송무담당관 신광옥

법 무 부 장 관

31581

0064

공 란

공 란

공 란

공　　란

국 방 부 7602

관재 01237- 1313 795-6331 90. 11. 16.

수신 외무부장관

참조 미주국장

제목 과제상정 철회

1. 관재 01237-558 (90.5.14)의 관련입니다.

2. 위호로 과제상정한 동두천시 하천 개수공사와 관련한 주한미군 훈련장 (7X-27)부지 약 2.19 에이카 해제요청은 과제 2700호의 양해각서 합의로 더 이상 협의할 필요가 없게되었읍니다.

3. 따라서, 본건 과제상정은 철회하오니 시설구역분과위원회의 새로운 과제로 위촉하지말도록 조치하여 주시기 바랍니다. 끝.

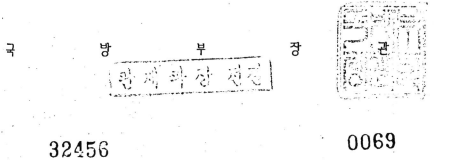

발송 1990.11.17 국방부

국 방 부 장 관

관재과장 전결

32456 0069

기안

국 방 부

관재 01237-1385　　795-6331　　90. 11. 20.

수신 외무부장관

참조 미주국장

제목 과제상정

1. 우리부는 민원인으로 부터 의정부시 의정부동 및 가능동 소재 주한미군과 협의하기 위하여 SOFA 합동위원회에 과제상정하오니 시설구역분과위원회 과제로 위촉하여 주시기 바랍니다.

[redacted]

나. 내 용 : 의정부시 의정부동 및 가능동 소재 주한미군용 전주 4기 이설. 끝.

32622

국 방 부 장

0070

국 방 부

관재 01237-1388 795-6331 90. 11. 20.

수신 외무부장관

참조 미주국장

제목 과제상정 의뢰

1. 우리부는 전쟁기념사업회로 부터 서울 용산구 용산동 소재 구 육군본부 자리에 "전쟁기념관" 건립에 따른 미8군 영내 개천복개와 미8군 출입문 활용문제를 제의 받은바 있읍니다.

2. 위 제의에 따른 미8군 메인포스트내의 개천을 복개한후 전쟁기념사업회에서 사용하는 문제와 (약 1.3 에이카) 출입문 조정 및 활용문제를 시설구역분과위원회 과제로 위촉하여 주시기 바랍니다. 끝.

32824

국 방 부 장

0071

기안

국 방 부

관제 01237-1450 795-6331 '90. 11. 30.

수신 외무부장관

참조 미주국장

제목 과제상정

1. 우리부는 현재 방위비 분담사업의 일환으로 미군용 케이블 공사를 추진중에 있습니다.

2. 이와 별도로 한국 데이타 통신 주식회사에서는 포항 - 서울간 미군 송유관로 부지에 광케이블을 첨가 시설하여 국방지휘 통신축선과 공용하자는 제의가 있어 이를 미측과 협의 추진하고자 하니, 시설구역 분과위원회 과제로 위촉하여 주시기 바랍니다. 끝.

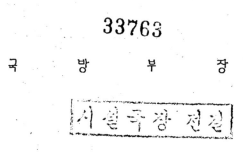

1990. 11. 30 국방부

33763

국 방 부 장

시설국장 전결

0072

76 ㅇㄹ

국　　　방　　　부

관재 01237- 1451　　　795-6331　　　90. 11. 30.

수신 외무부장관

제목 미주국장

제목 과제상정 의뢰

1. 우리부는 부산지방 국토관리청으로부터 영천-고경간 도로포장공사에 저촉되는 주한미군 송유관(MP24)이설 및 보호협의를 받고, 주한미군과 지속적인 협의를 위하여 SOFA 합동위원회에 과제 상정하오니 시설구역 분과위원회 과제로 위촉하여 주시기 바랍니다. 끝.

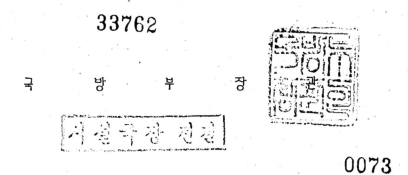

발송 1990. 11. 30 국방부

33762

국　　방　　부　　장

국방부장관인

시설국장 전결

0073

공 란

공 란

공 란

공 란

국 방 부

관제 01237- 1469 795-6331 90. 12. 6.

수신 외무부장관

참조 미주국장

제목 과제상정 의뢰

1. 우리부는 대구시 남구청으로 부터 동청 관내 한우아파트-영대 네거리간 도시계획도로 개설구간에 편입된 주한미군사 시설(캠프워카)의 일부 해제반환 요청 받고, 주한미군과의 지속적인 협의를 위하여 SOFA 합동위원회에 과제상정하오니 시설분과위원회 과제로 위촉하여 주시기 바랍니다. 끝.

발송 1990.12.06 국방부

34447

국 방 부 장

시설국장 전결

0078

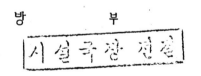

국 방 부

관제 01237-1475 795-6331 90. 12. 7.

수신 외무부장관

참조 미주국장

제목 과제상정

1. 주한미군 통신케이블 이설에 관한 한미 협의를 위하여 아래와 같이 합동위원회에 과제상정하오니 시설구역 분과위원회 과제로 위촉하여 주시기 바랍니다.

가. 과제 1

1) 요청기관 : 한국도로공사

2) 내 용 : 경부고속도로 양재-수원간 도로확장공사에 저촉되는 주한미군 통신케이블 이설

나. 과제 2

1) 요청기관 : 한국 토지개발공사

2) 내 용 : 분당지역 택지개발 사업에 저촉되는 주한미군 통신케이블 약 4Km이설. 끝.

발송 1990.12.07 국방부

국 방 부 장 관

관제과장 전결

34652 0079

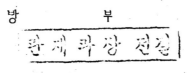

가

국 방 부

관제 01237-1495 795-6331 90. 12. 12.

수신 외무부장관

참조 미주국장

제목 과제상정

1. 우리부는 연기축산업협동조합으로 부터 조치원 가축시장 개설사업에 저촉되는 주한미군 송유관 보호요청을 받고, 이를 주한미군과 협의하기 위하여 SOFA 합동위원회에 과제상정하오니 시설구역분과위원회 과제로 위촉하여주시기 바랍니다. 끝.

발송 1990. 12. 12 국방부

국 방 부 장 관

관제과장 전결

34971 0080

" 법지켜 보호받고 질서지켜 혼란막자 "

국 방 부

관재 01237-1535 795-6331 90. 12. 19.

수신 외무부장관

참조 미주국장

제목 과제상정

1. 포항시는 동시 장성동 도로확장계획에 저촉되는 주한미군용 전주17본을 신설 도로계획선에 맞게 이설하고자 협의요청하여 왔읍니다.

2. 본건에 대하여 주한미군과 세부적인 협의를 위하여 SOFA합동위원회에 과제상정하오니 시설구역분과위원회 과제로 위촉하여 주시기 바랍니다.

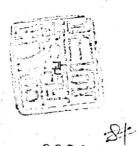

1990.12.20 국방부

접수일시	1990.12.21	
처리과	35672	

국 방 부 장 관

한재관장 전결

0081

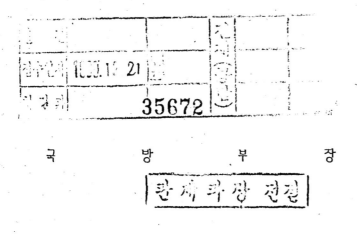

가인

대 한 민 국

상 공 부

통 정 20294 ~ 6 503~9445 1991. 1. 4

수 신 외무부장관

참 조 미주국장

제 목 SOFA 합동위 상무분과 위원장 변경통보

SOFA 합동위원회 상무분과위원회 한국측위원장이 '90. 12. 28부로 장석환 (張石煥, Chang Sokan) 국장으로 변경되었음을 통보하니 귀 업무에 참고하시기 바랍니다. 끝.

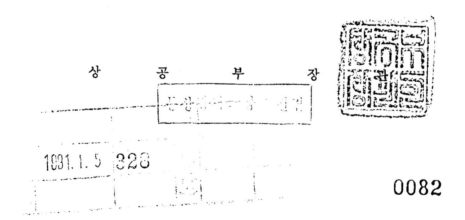

1991. 1. 04
상공부

상 공 부 장 관

1991. 1. 5 328

0082

공 란

공 란

공 란

공 란

공　　　란

공 란

공 란

공 란

공　　란

공 란

⊐ROCEDURES FOR OPERATION OF THE US-ROK JOINT COMMITTEE

The Republic of Korea and the United States Representatives have agreed upon the following procedures for the operation of the Republic of Korea-United States Joint Committee:

1. The Joint Committee will hold regularly scheduled weekly meetings in the first months after the Status of Forces Agreement enters into force, but either the US or the ROK Joint Committee Representative may call additional sessions of the Joint Committee at any time.

2. The Chairmanship of the Joint Committee meetings will be rotated between the ROK and the US Representatives, with the ROK Representative presiding at the first meeting and the US Representative presiding at the second meeting, etc.

3. When the ROK Representative presides at the meeting, it will be held in a ROK Government conference room; when the US Representative serves as the Chairman, the meeting will be held in the US SOFA Conference Room, Building 2370, Yongsan (near the USFK Command Building).

4. The ROK Government accepts the responsibility for maintaining the official index of Joint Committee actions and agreements. In turn, the US agrees to assume the responsibility for the preparation of the official Joint Committee meeting minutes, for coordinating with the ROK to obtain joint US-ROK approval for these minutes, and for their publication (with the ROK Government being furnished the desired number of copies).

5. The official minutes of the Joint Committee meetings will be considered as official documents pertaining to both Governments and will not be released without mutual agreement. In addition, no press releases will be issued following a US-ROK Joint Committee meeting, or following any action of the Joint Committee, without mutual agreement.

6. The Joint Committee procedures will have the flexibility necessary for effective functioning of the Joint Committee in implementation of the SOFA. Provision will be made for Joint Committee exigency actions, to be accomplished without a formal Joint Committee meeting, by mutual agreement of the US and ROK Representatives. Such emergency action will be later recorded in the official minutes of a US-ROK Joint Committee meeting. However, written memoranda will normally be the media utilized for presentation of official positions of the US and ROK Representatives and for the presentation of recommendations of subcommittees to the Joint Committee.

1st JC - Incl 4
9 Feb 67

Procedures for JC & SubC
Art VIII: Civilians/Depnds

PROCEDURES FOR
OPERATION OF THE US-ROK JOINT COMMITTEE SUBCOMMITTEES

The Republic of Korea and the United States Representatives have agreed that the United States-Republic of Korea Joint Committee establish US-ROK subcommittees to assist the Joint Committee and that the following procedures will be used in the operation of these subcommittees:

1. The Joint Committee will organize subcommittees for the purpose of giving advice and making recommendations on technical matters to the Joint Committee. Subcommittees will give advice and make recommendations only on those matters specifically referred to them by the Joint Committee.

2. All recommendations of subcommittees and other subordinate elements of the US-ROK Joint Committee must be approved by the Joint Committee before they become effective.

3. Each Joint Committee subcommittee will have a US and a ROK chairman. Chairmanship of the Joint Committee subcommittee meetings should be rotated between the ROK and the US chairmen, with the ROK chairman presiding at the first meeting, the US chairman at the second meeting, etc.

4. When the ROK chairman presides at a meeting, it will usually be held in a ROK Government conference room; when the US chairman presides, the meeting will usually be held in the US SOFA Conference Room, Building 2370, Yongsan (near the USFK Command Building).

5. The official minutes and other documents of the Joint Committee subcommittees will be considered as official documents pertaining to both Governments, and will not be publicly released by the subcommittees.

6. No press releases will be issued following US-ROK Joint Committee subcommittee meetings without prior agreement of the US and ROK Joint Committee Representatives.

7. The format for submitting recommendations from US-ROK Joint Committee subcommittees to the Joint Committee shall be as follows:

a. Subcommittee name.

1st JC - Incl 5
9 Feb 67

0094 54

see 86th mtg 1973

b. Subcommittee members - United States and Republic of Korea.

c. Subject of recommendation.

d. The recommendation, in full, with reference to appropriate articles and sections of the Status of Forces Agreement. (In the event of disagreement between the United States and the Korean components of the subcommittee, this paragraph should present both the United States recommendation and the Korean recommendation, the portions agreed upon and the portions in disagreement, with reference to appropriate articles and sections of the Status of Forces Agreement.)

e. Security classification, if any.

f. Signature of both the United States and the Republic of Korea subcommittee chairmen.

8. If the Joint Committee approves a recommendation of a US-ROK Joint Committee subcommittee, such Joint Committee approval is noted below the signature of subcommittee chairmen, along with the date of Joint Committee meeting. The US and the ROK Representatives sign each approved subcommittee recommendation.

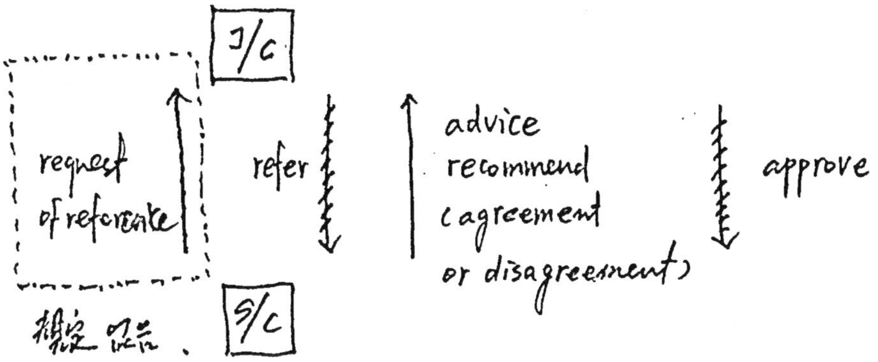

1st JC - Incl 5
9 Feb 67

Art VIII : Civilians/Depdts

SAMPLE

ROK-US JOINT COMMITTEE - US COMPONENT

COMMITTEE POSITION	DUTY TITLE/POSITION	TELEPHONE EXCHANGE
US REPRESENTATIVE		
Lt Gen Ronald R. Fogleman United States Air Force	Deputy Commander US Forces Korea	723-5239 YS 784-7001 OS
ALTERNATE REPRESENTATIVE		
Col Samuel N. Bole United States Air Force	Special Assistant to the Deputy Commander	723-6033 YS
DEPUTY REPRESENTATIVES		
COL Norman G. Cooper United States Army	Judge Advocate	723-6033
CAPT Robert M. Werner United States Navy	Chief of Staff US Naval Forces Korea	723-4891 YS
POLITICAL ADVISOR		
Mr. Richard A. Christenson	First Secretary Political Section American Embassy, Seoul	721-4133 AE
SECRETARY		
Dr. Carroll B. Hodges	Special Assistant to the Deputy Commander US Forces Korea	723-6046 YS 793-0283 SC
ALTERNATE SECRETARY		
Maj Malcolm H. Perkins United States Air Force	Office of the Deputy Cdr US Forces Korea	723-6374 YS
ASSISTANT SECRETARY		
Mr. James T. Burns, Jr.	Office of the Deputy Cdr US Forces Korea	723-7718 YS 793-0283 SC
INTERPRETER		
Mr. Mun Chae Sik	Office of the Deputy Cdr US Forces Korea	723-7719 YS 793-0283 SC

第 28 條

合 同 委 員 會

1. 달리 規定한 境遇를 除外하고는 本協定의 施行에 關한 相互協議를 必要로 하는 모든 事項에 關한 大韓民國 政府와 合衆國 政府間의 協議機關으로서 合同委員會를 設置한다. 特히, 合同 委員會는 本 協定의 目的을 遂行하기 爲하여 合衆國의 使用에 所要되는 大韓民國 안의 施設과 區域을 決定하는 協議機關으로서 役割한다.

2. 合同委員會는 大韓民國 政府 代表 1名과 合衆國 政府 代表 1名으로 構成하고, 各 代表는 1名 또는 그 以上의 代理人과 職員團을 둔다. 合同委員會는 그 自體의 節次 規則을 定하고, 또한 必要한 補助 機關과 事務 機關을 設置한다. 合同 委員會는 大韓民國 政府 또는 合衆國 政府 中의 어느 一方 政府 代表의 要請이 있을 때에는 어느 때라도 即時 會合할 수 있도록 組織되어야 한다.

3. 合同委員會가 어떠한 問題를 解決할 수 없을 때에는 同委員會는 이 問題를 適切한 經路를 通하여 그 以上의 檢討를 講究하기 爲하여 各己 政府에 回附하여야 한다.

第28條에 對한 合意議事錄

第1項 第1段에서 規定하고 있는 例外는 第3條 第2項 (나) 및 (다)에만 關聯된다.

ARTICLE XXVIII

Joint Committee

1. A Joint Committee shall be established as the means for consultation between the Government of the United States and [redacted] Government of the Republic of Korea on all matters requiring mutual consultation regarding the implementation of this Agreement except where otherwise provided. In particular, the Joint Committee shall serve as the means for consultation in determining the facilities and areas in the Republic of Korea which are required for the use of the United States in carrying out the purposes of this Agreement.

2. The Joint Committee shall be composed of a representative of the Government of the United States and a representative of the Government of the Republic of Korea. each of whom shall have one or more deputies and a staff. The Joint Committee shall determine its own procedures, and arrange for such auxiliary organs and administrative services as may be required. The Joint Committee shall be so organized that it may meet immediately at [illegible] time at the request of the representative of either the Government of the United States or the Government of the Republic of Korea.

3. If the Joint Committee is unable to resolve any matter, it shall refer that matter to the respective Governments for further consideration through appropriate channels.

(Agreed minutes) ARTICLE XXVIII

The exception provided for in the first sentence of paragraph 1 is relevant only to paragraph 2, subparagraphs (b) and (c) of Article III.

0097

항공시설관리규칙 〔1969. 7.18 교통부령제 335 호 한글화〕

교통부령 제 352 호 1969. 9.15개정	교통부령 제 444 호 1973. 4.24개정
교통부령 제 470 호 1974. 1.21	교통부령 제 523 호 1976. 1.14
교통부령 제 547 호 1976.12.27	교통부령 제 578 호 1977. 8.12
교통부령 제 590 호 1978. 3. 6	교통부령 제 665 호 1980. 6.20
교통부령 제 703 호 1981. 4.30	교통부령 제 730 호 1982. 1.29
교통부령 제 748 호 1982.11.23	교통부령 제 761 호 1983. 4.29
교통부령 제 788 호 1984. 7.11	교통부령 제 846 호 1986.12.22
교통부령 제 873 호 1988. 1. 6	교통부령 제 883 호 1988. 5.18
	교통부령 제 920 호 1990. 2. 1

제 1 조(목적) 이 규칙은 항공시설의 관리와 규제를 행함으로써 항공시설을 능률적으로 운영하고 그 질서를 유지하기 위하여 필요한 사항을 정함을 목적으로 한다.

제 2 조(정의) 이 규칙에서 "항공시설"이라함은 교통부 및 국제공항관리공단법에 의한 국제공항관리공단(이하 "공단"이라 한다)이 관리 운영하는 비행장(국제공항을 포함한다. 이하 같다)의 여객청사, 화물청사, 활주로, 계류장, 주차장, 관제통신 및 항공보안시설과 그 부대시설 및 지원시설을 말한다.
〈개정 76.1.19 교통령 523, 전문개정 80.6.20 교통령 665〉

제 3 조(적용제외) 항공시설을 군용항공기가 이용하는 경우에는 제 4 조, 제 5 조, 제 7 조 내지 제 9 조, 제 12 조 내지 제 18 조, 제 23 조 내지 제 25 조, 제 27 조의 규정은 이를 적용하지 아니한다.

제 4 조(입장의 제한) ①비행장에 입장하고자 하는 자는 비행장 입구에서 입장표의 교부를 받아야 한다.
다만, 다음 각 호의 1에 해당하는 자는 예외로 한다〈개정84.7.11 교통령 788〉
1. 항공기 승무원 및 여객
2. 비행장 근무하는 자로서 비행장장(국제공항장을 포함한다. 이하같다)이 발행하는 입장증을 가진 자.
3. 비행장장이 특히 허가한 자.

1-3-1 〈추2〉

0098

④다음의 경우에[redacted] 착륙료, 항공보안시설이용료, 정류료, 격납고사용료, 조명료, 주차장사용료, 국제여객공항이용료, 계류장사용료와 환송대 입장료를 면제할 수 있다.

〈개정 76.1.19 교통령 523, 76.12.27 교통령 547, 81.4.30 교통령 703〉

1. 이륙후 1시간 이내에 부득이한 사유로 이륙한 비행장에 다시 발착하거나 부득이한 사유로 어느 비행장에 불시착하거나 불시착후 최초로 이륙하는 경우

2. 외교상의 목적 또는 공용에 사용되는 항공기와 시험비행 또는 교육법 제109조의 규정에 의한 대학이나 이와 동등 이상의 교육기관에서 실시하는 조종훈련을 위한 항공기의 착륙 및 이륙의 경우〈개정 84.7.11 교통령 788〉

3. 행정상의 필요에 의하여 명하여진 착륙 및 이륙의 경우

4. 외교상의 목적으로 사용되는 자동차와 비행장내에 소재하는 행정기관 소속의 자동차의 주차장사용료 및 계류장사용료.

5. 외교관여권소지자와 2세미만의 소아 또는 대한민국에 주둔하는 국제연합군 소속의 군인, 군무원과 우리나라를 통과하는 여객이 공항의 폐쇄 또는 기상관계로 인하여 항공기의 출발이 지연되거나 다른 항공기와의 접속이 불가능하여 부득이 공항보세구역을 벗어나는 여객에 대한 국제여객공항이용료〈개정 81.4.30 교통령 703〉

6. 6세 미만에 대한 환송대 입장료

7. 항공시설의 건설, 개량, 보수 및 유지를 위하여 출입하는 차량 및 장비에 대한 주차장사용료 및 계류장 사용료〈신설 81.4.30 교통령 703〉.

⑤입장권의 개찰후 일기의 불순 기타 부득이한 사유로 항공기가 이륙 또는 착륙하지 못하여 결항된 경우에 있어서 입장료 환불 요건이 있을 때에는 당해 비행장장 또는 공단이사장은 결항을 확인한 후 입장료의 전액을 환불할 수 있다〈개정 80.6.20 교통령 665〉.

⑥국제여객공항이용료는 탑승절차를 취할 때에 당해 항공운송사업자를 거쳐 비행장장 또는 공단이사장에게 납부하여야 한다〈개정 80.6.20 교통령 665〉.

⑦특별대합실사용료는 당해 항공기가 결항한 때에는 이를 징수하지 아니한다〈개정 80.6.20 교통령 665〉

1-3-5

〈추2〉

0093

REGULATIONS OF MANAGEMENT OF AVIATION FACILITIES

(Ministry of Transportation Order #335)

(18 July 1969)

(EXCERPTS)

(4) The following passengers may be exempted from payment of the airport service charge:

5. Persons who are in possession of diplomatic passport; infants who are under two years old; and the servicemembers and civilian components of the United Nations forces stationed in the Republic of Korea.

0100

1. 25 전달

JOINT COMMITTEE
UNDER
THE REPUBLIC OF KOREA AND THE UNITED STATES
STATUS OF FORCES AGREEMENT

January 24, 1991

Dr. Carroll B.Hodges
U.S Secretary
ROK-U.S. Joint Committee

Dear Dr. Hodges,

Attached is a memorandum for the Facilities and Areas Subcommittee requesting release of real estate related to Seoul Metropolitan Area facilities and areas relocation. An MOA regarding this issue has been signed between the Minister of National Defense of the ROK and the USFK Commander on June 25, 1990.

I respectfully request that the U.S. Representative review and approve the ROK request as an exigent action. A formal record of approval of this action will be entered into record at the next regular Joint Committee Meeting.

Sincerely,

Song Min Soon
ROK Secretary
ROK-U.S. Joint Committee

0101

공 란

가인

건 설 부

수관 30343-2114 503-7337 1991. 1. 25.
(3년)

수신 외무부 장관

참조 미주국장

제목 공공용역 분과위원회 위원변경 통보

SOFA와 관련한 공공용역 분과 위원회 위원이 다음과 같이 변경되었기 통보합니다.

당 초	변 경	변 경 일 자
건설부 상하수도국 수도관리과장 이 두 헌	건설부 상하수도국 수도관리과장 윤 유 학	'91. 1. 21.

발신용 1991. 1. 25 전신과

끝.

건 설 부 장

수도관리과장 전결

1991. 1 29
2664
결재(공람)

0103

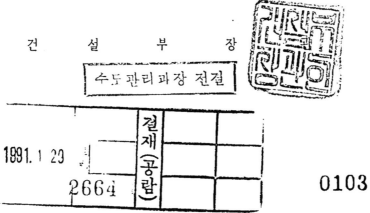

공 란

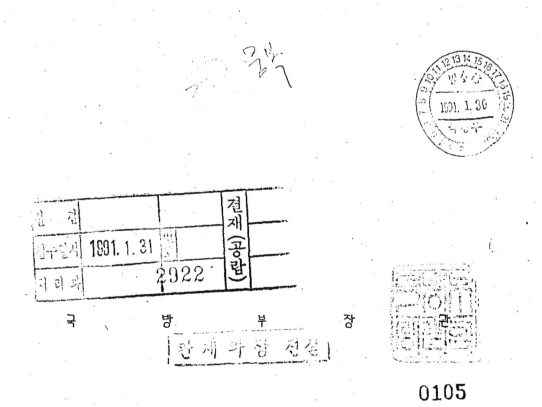

" 법지켜 보호받고 질서지켜 혼란막자 "

국 방 부

관재 01237 - 91 795-6331 91. 1. 29.

수신 외무부장관

참조 미주국장

제목 과제상정

1. 우리부는 한국토지개발공사로부터 분당지역 택지개발 사업에 따른 주한 미군 통신케이블 약 4 Km 정도 보호 및 이설협의 요청을 받았습니다.

2. 상기 건의 한·미간 계속 협의를 위하여 SOFA 합동위원회에 과제상정 의뢰하오니 이를 시설구역분과위원회의 과제로 위촉바랍니다. 끝.

분 류			결재(공람)
접수일시	1991. 1. 31		
처리과	2922		

국 방 부 장 관

관재과장 전결

0105

공 란

대 한 민 국

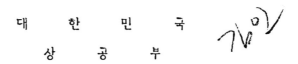

상 공 부

통 정	20294 - 255	503 - 9445	1991. 1. 29

수 신 외무부장관

참 조 미주국장

제 목 SOFA 합동위 상무분과 위원회 명단 통보

SOFA 합동위 상무분과위원회 한국측 명단을 별첨과 같이 통보하니 " 위원회 및 분과위원회 관계관 명단" 변경등 귀업무에 참고하여 주시기 바랍니다.

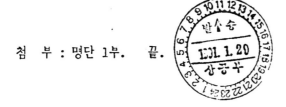

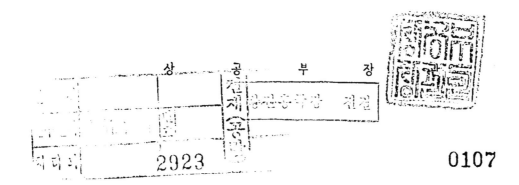

첨 부 : 명단 1부. 끝.

발송순 1991. 1. 30 상공부

상 공 부 장

2923

0107

상무분과 위원회 - 한국측

위 원 장

장 석 환	상공부 통상진흥국장	503 - 9442

교체 위원장

최 홍 건	상공부 통상협력관	503 - 9443

간 사

신 동 오	상공부 통상정책과장	503 - 9444

부 간 사

심 성 근	상공부 통상진흥국 통상정책과	503 - 9445

위 원

예 계 해	내무부 치안본부 외사부장	313 - 0848
신 동 규	재무부 세제국 국제조세과장	504 - 3676
구 창 덕	법무부 출입국관리국 입국심사과장	503 - 7095
김 광 식	상공부 상역국 무역정책과장	503 - 9432
정 기 수	상공부 상역국 수입과장	503 - 9440
김 원 배	노동부 노정국 노정과장	503 - 9730
김 인 철	외무부 미주국 안보과	720 - 2324

0108

COMMERCE SUBCOMMITTEE-ROK COMPONENT

CHAIRMAN		TELEPHONE EXCHANGE
Mr. Chang Sokan	Director-General, Int'l Trade Promotion Bureau Ministry of Trade and Industry	503 - 9442
ALTERNATE CHAIRMAN		
Mr. Choe Hong Geon	Director-General Trade Cooperation Bureau Ministry of Trade and Industry	503 - 9443
SECRETARY		
Mr. Shin Dong Oh	Director, Int'l Trade Policy Division Int'l Trade Promotion Bureau Ministry of Trade and Industry	503 - 9444
ASSISTANT SECRETARY		
Mr. Shim Soung Kun	Deputy Director Int'l Trade Policy Division Int'l Trade Promotion Bureau Ministry of Trade and Industry	503 - 9445
MEMBERS		
Mr. Yae Kye Hae	Superintendent General, Foreign Affairs Bureau Korean National Police Headquarters Ministry of Home Affairs	313 - 0848

0103

Mr. Shin Dong Kyu	Director, International Tax Division Tax Bureau Ministry of Finance	504 - 3676
Mr. Koo Chang Deok	Director, Entry Control Division Bureau of Immigration Ministry of Justice	503 - 7095
Mr. Kim Gwang Shik	Director, Trade Policy Division Trade Bureau Ministry of Trade and Industry	503 - 9432
Mr. Chung Kee Soo	Director, Import Division Trade Bureau Ministry of Trade and Industry	503 - 9440
Mr. Kim Won Bae	Director, Labor Policy Division Bureau of Labor Policy Ministry of Labor	503 - 9730
Mr. Kim In Chul	National Security Division American Affairs Bureau Ministry of Foreign Affairs	720 - 2324

0110

공 란

공 란

공 란

공 란

공　　　　란

공 란

공　　　　　란

공 란

공 란

공 란

협조문용지

			결재	담 당	과 장	심의관
분류기호 문서번호	미안 01225- 10	(전화 720-2324)				
시행일자	1991. 2 .20 .			김인철		
수　　신	총무과장(서무)	발　신	미주국장 (서명)			
제　　목	청사 출입증 발급					

당국 SOFA 합동위원회 운영 업무에 필요하니 아래 사람에 대한 청사 출입증 발급에 필요한 조치를 취해 주시기 바랍니다.

o 성　명 : James T. Burns Jr.

o Social Security No.: 104-36-5765

o 소　속 : 주한미군 부사령관 특별 보좌관실 (SOFA 합동위 간사 사무실)

o 직　위 : SOFA 합동위 미측 부간사

첨　부 : SOFA 합동위 미측 간사 요청 서한 사본 1부.　　끝.

0121

공 란

기안

국 방 부

관재 01237- 164 795 - 6331 91. 2. 21.

수신 외무부장관

참조 미주국장

제목 과제상정 의뢰

1. 우리부는 한국가스공사에서 시행하는 대전-평택간 천연가스 공급 배관 건설공사에 저촉되는 주한미군용 송유관 보호에 대하여 주한미군측과 협의하기 위하여 SOFA합동위원회에 과제상정하오니 시설구역분과위원회 과제로 위촉하여 주시기 바랍니다. 끝.

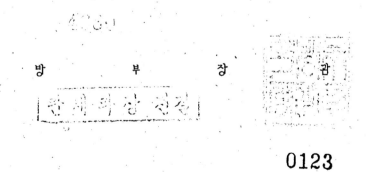

1991. 2. 21

35

국 방 부 장 관

0123

국 방 부

관재 01237-198 795-6331 91. 3. 5.

수신 외무부장관

참조 미주국장

제목 송유관 보호 협의

1. 우리부는 금릉군청으로부터 금릉군 남면 부상리 821-3번지상의 미군 송유관이 공장 진입로와 저촉이되어 보호 처리하겠다는 협조 의뢰가 있었습니다.

2. 위 사안을 미측과 정식 협의하고자 SOFA 시설구역 분과위원회 과제로 산정의뢰 하오니 이를 위촉하여 주시기 바랍니다. 끝.

국 방 부 장 관

5769 0124

국 방 부

관제 01237-213 795-6331 91. 3. 8.

수신 외무부장관

참조 미주국장

제목 과제상정 의뢰

1. 우리부는 의정부시로 부터 관내 금오동 25-7번지상에 주한미군 송유관이 있어 이를 보호 케이싱한후 단지내 도로로 사용할수 있도록 협조요청 받았읍니다.

2. 위 내용을 주한미군측과 정식협의할수 있도록 SOFA 합동위원회에 과제상정 의뢰하오니 시설구역분과위원회 과제로 위촉하여 주시기 바랍니다. 끝.

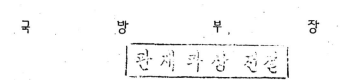

국 방 부 장 관

관제과장 전결

0428 0125

공 란

공 란

공 란

공 란

· 기안

국 방 부

관제 01237-239 795-6331 91. 3. 13.

수신 외무부장관

참조 미주국장

제목 송유관 보호협의

1. 우리부는 한국도로공사로부터 구리-퇴계원간 고속도로 건설과 관련하여 구리 인터체인지에 저촉되고있는 미군송유관의 보호 또는 이설협의 요청을 받았읍니다.

2. 위 송유관 보호문제를 SOFA 합동위원회에 과제상정하오니 미측과 정식 협의가 되도록 시설구역분과위원회 과제로 위촉하여 주시기 바랍니다. 끝.

1991. 3. 14

국 방 부 장 관

0130

676

조
길인 > ?

국 방 부

관재 01237.- 252 795-6331 91. 3. 15.

수신 외무부장관

참조 미주국장

제목 송유관 보호 협의

1. 우리부는 부산지방국토관리청으로부터 포항-청하간 도로확장공사에 저촉이 되는 미군송유관의 보호협의 요청을 받았읍니다.

2. 위 협의사안을 주한미군측과 계속협의하기 위해 SOFA 합동위원회에 과제상정하고자 하니 시설구역분과위원회 과제로 위촉하여 주시기 바랍니다. 끝.

1991. 3. 1
국방부

국 방 부 장 관

관제과장 전결

7033

0131

길인

국 방 부

관재 22410-286 795-6331 91. 3. 25.

수신 외무부장관

참조 미주국장

제목 과제상정

1. 우리부 예하 공군 제30방공 관제단은 급수문제에 직면하고 있어 주한미군 화악산 심정(취득번호 : K-E- 1024)을 주한미군과 공동사용 할 것을 협의하고 있습니다.

2. 본건에 대한 한.미간 세부적인 협의를 위하여 SOFA 합동위원회에 과제 상정하오니 시설구역 분과위원회 과제로 위촉하여 주시기 바랍니다. 끝.

1991. 3. 26

8075

국 방 부 장 관

0132

김인

국　　　방　　　부

관재 24460-305　　　795-6331　　　91. 3. 28.

수신　외무부장관

참조　미주국장

제목　과제상정

1. 우리부는 양주군으로부터 동군 남방 - 유양간 도로 확장공사에 저촉되는 주한미군용 통신케이블 이설 요청을 받았습니다.

2. 본건에 대하여 주한미군측과 협의하기 위하여 SOFA 합동위원회에 과제상정하오니 시설구역 분과위원회 과제로 위촉하여 주시기 바랍니다. 끝.

1991. 3. 28

국　방　부　장　관

8375

0133

국 방 부

관재 01237-316 (795-6331) 91. 4. 4.

수신 외무부장관

참조 미주국장

제목 과제상정 의뢰

1. 건설부 수도권 수도건설사무소는 수도권 광역 상수도사업에 저촉되는 강남구 양재동 및 경기도 과천시 소재 주한미군 송유관을 보호요청하고 있읍니다.

2. 본건에 대한 주한미군측과 세부적인 협의를 위하여 SOFA합동위원회에 과제상정하오니 시설구역분과위원회의 과제로 위촉하여 주시기 바랍니다. 끝.

1991. 4. 04

국 방 부 장 관

9170

0134

검인

농 림 수 산 부

국협20333-334 503-7227 1991. 4. 12.

수신 외무부장관

제목 SOFA/식물검역 임시 분과위원회 대표 명단 통보

1. 관련 : 방역 27151 -222 ('90. 4. 10)

2. 미국측 SOFA합동위 간사인 Mr. Hodges로 부터 분과위원회 준비에 필요한 한국측 대표단 명단을 알려달라는 서신 요청에 따라 새로 변경된 아측대표단 명단을 별첨과 같이 통보하오니 미측에 전달될 수 있도록 협조하여 주시기 바랍니다.

첨부 1. SOFA/식물검역 임시 분과위원회 한국측 명단 (국.여문) 1부.

2. Mr. Hodges 서신 1부. 끝.

발송 1991. 4. 12 농림수산부

농 림 수 산 부 장 관

국제협력담당관 전결

10392

0135

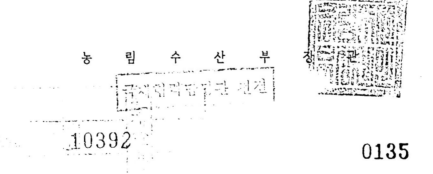

SOFA /식물검역 임시분과 위원회 한국측 대표 명단

위원장	**전화번호**
안 신 환 국립식물검역소장	(0343)49-0523
교체위원장	
홍 언식 농림수산부 식물방역과장	503- 7255
간 사	
서 기호 국립식물검역소 국제검역정보과장	(0343)45-1223
위 원	
김광용 농림수산부 식물방역과 검역주무	503 - 7255
박창용 국립식물검역소 국제검역정보과 제1계주무	(0343)46-1926
신현포 " 조사연구과 이화학주무	(0343)45-1225
공효상 " 검역과 기획주무	(0343)49-0524
김진성 " 국제검역정보과	(0343)46-1926
심성섭 " 인천지소장	(032) 72-1540
조병재 외무부 안보과	720-2324

0136

AD HOC SUBCOMMITTEE ON PLANT QUARANTINE

(ROK COMPONENT)

Chairman		Telephone Exchange
Mr, AHAN Sin Hwan	Director General National Plant Quarantine Service	(0343)49-0523

Alternate Chairman

Mr. HONG In Shik	Director Plant Protection Div., MAFF	503-7255

Secretary

Mr. SUH Ki Ho	Director Int'l. Quarantine Information Div. , NPQS	(0343)45-1223

Members

Mr. KIM Kwang-Woong	Assistant Director Plant Protection Div., MAFF	503-7255
Mr. PARK Chang Yong	Assistant Director Int'l.Quarantine Information Div.,NPQS	(0343)46-1926
Mr.SHIN Hyun Po	Assistant Director Investigation & Research Div., NPQS	(0343)45-1225
Mr. Kong Hyo Sang	Assistant Director Quarantine Div.,NPQS	(0343)49-0524
Mr.KIM Jin Seong	Plant Quarantine Officer Int'l .Quarantine Information Div.,NPQS	(0343)46-1926
Mr. SHIM Seong Seop	Director Incheon Branch, NPQS	(032) 72-1540
Mr. CHO Byoung Jae	National Security Division American Affairs Bureau Ministry of Foreign Affairs	720-2324

0137

공 란

13. AD HOC SUBCOMMITTEE ON PLANT QUARANTINE

ROK COMPONENT

		TELEPHONE EXCHANGE
CHAIRMAN		
Mr. ~~KIM Yun Sun~~ AHAN, SIN-HWAN	Director General National Plant Quarantine Office	(0343)49-0523 48-6429
ALTERNATE CHAIRMAN		
Mr. KIM Jung Kee	Director Plant Protection Div., MAFF	503-7255
SECRETARY		
Mr. ~~SHIN Seong Seop~~ SUH, KI-HO	Director, INTERNATIONAL QUARANTINE INFO SERVICE NATIONAL PLANT ~~Plant~~ Quarantine ~~Div.~~, NPQO	(0343)~~49-0524~~ 45-1223
MEMBERS		
Mr. KIM Min Jae	Assistant Director Plant Protection Div., MAFF	503-7255
Mr. PARK Chang Yong	Assistant Director Plant Quarantine Div., NPQO	(0343)49-0524
Mr. KIM Young Il	Assistant Director Plant Quarantine Div., NPQO	(0343)49-0524
Mr. HAN Sang Jin	Technical Assistant in Plant Pathology Plant Quarantine Div., NPQO	(0343)49-0524
Mr. JIN Yong Tae	Director Inchon Branch, NPQO	(032)72-1540
Mr. SHIN Hyun Po	Director Seoul Branch, NPQO	664-3841
Mr. LEE Sang Hak	National Security Division American Affairs Bureau, Ministry of Foreign Affairs	720-2324, 2239

13. 식물검역위시분과위원회-미국측

위원장		**전화번호**
대령 윌리엄 제이. 파키 2세	주한미군 군수참모실	7913-4451
교체위원장		
대령 하워드 씨. 존슨 미육군	주한미군 수의관	7913-3338
간사		
대위 헥터 카스텔로 미공군	주한미군 군수참모실	7913-4453
위원		
캐롤 비. 하지스 박사	주한미군 부사령관 특별보좌관	7913-6048 793-0283
랄프 지포드	주한미대사관 농무관	732-2601 (교환: 4540)
포리 보렌드	제8지원대 연료보급과장	053-820-8313
중령 제임스 화간 미육군	주한미군 카미사리 극동지역 사령관	7918-5169
김 현수	주한미군 법무참모실	7913-6033
상사 제리 엠. 데이쿡 미공군	주한미군 오산기지 카미사리	0333-414-4403
참관인		
대위 안토니오 에스...꿈멘 미육군	주한미군 제19지원단	053-820-6453

김인

국 방 부

관제 01237 -3177 (795-6331) 91. 4. 18.

수신 외무부장관

참조 미주국장

제목 과제상정 의뢰

1. 우리부는 부산지방 국토관리청으로부터 경상북도내 고경 - 안강간 도로포장 공사에 저촉되는 주한미군 송유관에 대한 보호 및 이설요청을 받았습니다.

2. 본건에 대하여 주한미군과 협의하기 위하여 SOFA 합동위원회에 과제 상정하오니 시설구역 분과위원회 과제로 위촉하여 주시기 바랍니다.

끝.

1991. 4. 18

국 방 부 장

10896

0141

공 란

공 란

공 란

공 란

공 란

공　　　란

공 란

공 란

공 란

공　　　　란

공 란

공 란

공 란

공 란

공 란

공 란

공 란

공 란

공　　란

검토 - 검토

국 방 부

협력 24101- 765 (5731) 91. 5. 1
수신 수신처 참조 (1년)
제목 '91 방위비 분담 사업 면세 요구

1. 관련근거
   가. 주둔군 지위협정(SOFA)
   나. SOFA 제 5조에 대한 특별 협정(91.1.25)
   다. 제 22차 SCM 정책검토위 합의(90.11.14)
2. 위 근거 "다"에 의거 방위비 분담금을 지원토록 합의한 바 있음.
3. 방위비 분담 사업중 국방부에서 450만불 상당의 차량을 구매하여 주한미군을 지원하는 사업에 대하여 미측에서 SOFA 제 16조에 의거 면세 적용을 요구하여 그 내용을 첨부와 같이 통보하오니 업무에 참고 바랍니다.

첨부 : 주한미군 차량 지원시 면세 요구 내용 1부. 끝.

접수 1991. 5. 01 국방부

국 방 부 장 관

군수 협력 과장 전결

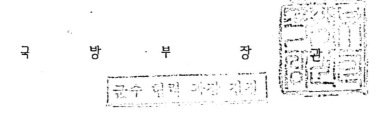

수신처 : 가20, 22, 44, 본18.

91 5 2

0161 12297

주한미군 차량지원관련 면세요구

1. 개 요

미측은 '91 방위비분담 사업중 주한미군용 차량지원(450만불)시 SOFA 제16조에 따른 면세 적용을 요구하여 그 진행 내용을 통보하는 내용

2. 경 위

'91.2	'91 주한미군 차량구매지원 MOA 협상시 면세 요구
'91.4.19	면세 적용 건을 미측에서 SOFA 합동위원회 제기
'91.4	재무부의견 접수 : 적용불가
'91.5	미순회대사(홈즈) 국방부 방문시 공식제기 예정 (정치적차원 해결시도)

3. 차량구매 지원 절차

차량구매 목록합의(국방부,주한미군) → 조달(국방군수본부) → 차량인도(주한미군)

※ 국방부에서 조달하여 미군 지원시에도 면세 적용 요구

4. 면세 관련 협정

o SOFA 제16조 3항(현지조달)

- 공인 조달기관을 포함한 합중국 군대가 대한민국 안에서 공용을 위하여 조달하는 자재, 수용품, 비품 및 용역 또는 합중국 군대의 최종 소비 사용을 위하여 조달하는 자재, 수용품, 비품 및 용역은 동 합중국 군대가 사전에 적절한 증명서를 제시하면 다음의 대한민국 조세가 면제된다.

0162

. 물 품 세

. 통 행 세

. 석유류세

. 전기 및 개스세

. 영 업 세

o SOFA 제16조에 대한 합의 의사록

- "공용을 위하여 조달하는 자재, 수용품, 비품 및 용역"이라 함은 합중국 군대 또는 그 공인 조달기관이 대한민국 공급자로부터 직접 조달함을 말하는 것으로 양해한다.

5. 부서별 주요 참고 사항

o 외무부 : SOFA 합동위원회 심의시 고려

o 재무부 : SOFA 재무분과위원회 심의시 고려

면세 결정시: 국내면세 절차 및 범위 결정시 고려

o 국세청 : 면세 결정시: 국내 면세 절차 및 범위 결정시 고려

o 정책기획관실 : 향후 방위비분담 정책방향 결정시 고려

0163

길인

경 제 기 획 원

조정 10311- 197 (503-9060) 1991. 5. 9.
수신 외무부장관
제목 주한 미군 적용 상수도 급수요율 개정에 관한 협의

1. 주한 미군에 적용되는 상수도 급수 요율 개정건에 대하여 별첨 영문(안) 사본과 같이 SOFA협정에 의한 협의를 미측공공용역분과위원장에게 제의하였음을 통보합니다.

첨부 1. 한국측 제의 영문(안) 사본 1부.
2. 건설부 공문 사본 1부. 끝.

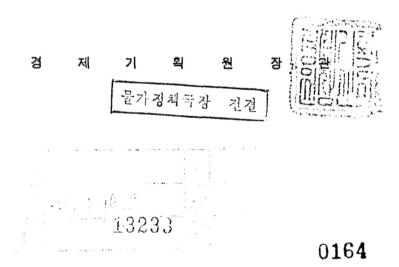

경 제 기 획 원 장 관

물가정책국장 전결

13233

0164

공 란

공 란

수도요금개정현황

지역	단계별	현행	개정	인상율
서울	공통	170	190	11.8%
부산	기본요금 (30㎥)	173	193	11.6%
	초과요금	240	300	25%
대구	기본요금 (20㎥)	150	170	13.3%
	초과요금	260	290	11.5%
인천	기본요금 (30㎥)	133	150	12.8%
	초과요금	190	220	15.8%
동두천	기본요금 (30㎥)	99	117	18.2%
	초과요금	150	180	20%
군산	기본요금 (30㎥)	140	170	21.4%
	초과요금	230	290	26.1%
의정부	기본요금 (30㎥)	186	229	23.1%
	초과요금	190	230	21.1%
부천	기본요금 (30㎥)	170	183	7.7%
	초과요금	285	320	10.9%
춘천	기본요금 (30㎥)	227	250	10.1%
	초과요금	350	390	11.4%
포항	기본요금 (30㎥)	120	157	30.8%
	초과요금	200	230	15%
원주	기본요금 (30㎥)	180	217	20.6%
	초과요금	260	280	7.7%
파주	기본요금 (30㎥)	126	147	16.7%
	초과요금	185	205	10.8%
송탄	기본요금 (30㎥)	174	214	22.5%
	초과요금	220	280	22.3%
수자원공사	기본요금	67.49	62	△8.1%
	계량요금	9.65	25.55	164.8%
	초과요금	92.04	124	34.7%

0167

기안

국 방 부

관재 01237-471 (795-6331) 91. 5. 10.

수신 외무부장관

참조 미주국장

제목 과제상정 의뢰

1. 경기도 오산시는 동시에서 시행하는 서부위회도로 개설사업구간(오산시 청학동-궐동)에 편입된 주한미군용 송유관 보호를 요청하였읍니다.

2. 본건에 대하여 주한미군과 협의하기 위하여 SOFA합동위원회 과제로 상정의뢰하오니 시설구역분과위원회 과제로 위촉하여 주시기 바랍니다. 끝.

1991. 5. 10

국 방 부 장 관

시설국장 전결

13569

0168

국 방 부

관제 01237- 497 (795-6331) 91. 5. 16.

수신 외무부장관

참조 미주국장

제목 과제상정 의뢰

1. 포항시는 동 시 우현동 도시계획도로공사에 저촉되는 주한미군용 철도선 보호협의를 요청하였읍니다.

2. 본건에 대한 주한미군과의 계속적인 협의를 위하여 SOFA위원회에 과제상정하오니 시설구역분과위원회 과제로 위촉하여 주시기 바랍니다. 끝.

1991. 5. 16
국방부

국 방 부 장 관

0169

공 란

공　　란

24061

기 안 용 지

분류기호 문서번호	미안01225-	(전화 : 720-2324)	시 행 상 특별취급	
보존기간	영구. 준영구 10. 5. 3. 1.	장 관		
수 신 처 보존기간				
시행일자	1991. 5. 24.			

보조기관	국 장	전 결	협조기관	문 서 통 제
	심의관			검열 1991. 5. 25 통제관
	과 장			발 송 인
기안책임자	김 인 철			

경 유 수 신 참 조	수신처 참조	발신명의		
제 목	SOFA 합동위원회 제169차 회의 개최			

1. 90.7 개최 예정이었던 SOFA 합동위원회 제169차 회의가 SOFA 개정 고섭으로 연기되어 왔었읍니다.

2. 91.2 동 고섭이 마무리되고 개정에 따른 후속 조치가 그간 이루어짐으로써 SOFA 합동위 협의가 정상화 됨에 따라 연기되었던 합동위 회의가 아래와 같이 개최될 예정입니다.

가. 일 시 : 1991.6.7(금). 16:00

/ 계속.... 0172

나. 장　　소 : 주한미군 용산영내 Dragon Hill Lodge 회의실

3. 이와관련, 각 위원께서는 참석하여 주시기 바라며 소관 분과위원회 별

협의 희망 안건이 있으면 통보하여 주시기 바랍니다.

수신처 : 재무부장관(관세국장), 법무부장관(법무실장, 검찰국장,

출입국관리국장), 국방부장관(정책기획관, 시설국장), 상공부장관

(통상진흥국장), 노동부장관(노정국장), 교통부장관(안전관리국장)

관세청장(심리기획관)　　　　　　　　끝.

0173

기안

교 통 부

차량 33150 - 6081 (392 - 9707) '91. 5. 28.

수신 수신처 참조

제목 SOFA 합동위원회 및 교통분과위원회 위원 교체 통보

SOFA 한미합동위원회 한국측 위원(교통부) 및 교통분과위원회 한국측 위원이 별첨과 같이 교체되었기 통보합니다.

첨부 교체명단(한국측) 1부. 끝.

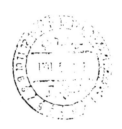

15627

교 통 부 장 안전관리국장 전결

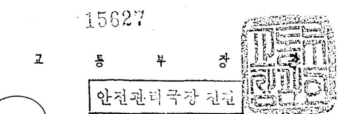

수신처 외무부(미주국 안보과), 한미합동위원회 미국측 간사(Dr Carroll B. Hodges), 교통분과위원회 미국측 간사(Maj Malcolm H. Perkins).

0174

o SOFA 한.미합동위원회(교통부)

구분	당 초		교 체		비 고
	직 위	성 명	직 위	성 명	
위원	안전관리 국장	김 경 회 (KIM KYUNG HOI)	안전관리 국장	김 창 원 (KIM, CHANG-WON)	'91.5.17

o SOFA 교통분과위원회(교통부)

구 분	직 위	성 명		비고
		당 초 (을)	교 체 (으로)	
위 원 장	안전관리국장	김 경 회 (KIM KYUNG HOI)	김 창 원 (KIM CHANG WON)	
교체위원장	항 공 국 장	이 헌 석 (LEE HEON SEOK)	장 부 시 (JANG BU SEE)	
위 원	서울지방항공 관리국 관리과장	이 환 건 (LEE HWAN GUAN)	김 수 용 (KIM SOO YOUNG)	

0175

50033 기 안 용 지

분류기호 문서번호	미이 01225-	(전화 : 720-2324)	시 행 상 특별취급
보존기간	영구.준영구. 10. 5. 3. 1.	장 관	
수 신 처 보존기간		(서명)	
시행일자	1991. 10. 9.		

보조기관	국 장	전 결	협조기관	문서통제
	심의관	(서명)		검열 1991. 10. 10 통제관
	과 장	(서명)		
기안책임자		조 준 혁		발송인 1991. 10. 1 외무부
경 유 수 신 참 조	수신처 참조		발신명의	
제 목	제169차 SOFA 합동위 의사록 송부			

1991. 6. 7 개최 제169차 SOFA 합동위원회 의사록을 별첨 송부하오니, 귀 업무에 참고하시기 바랍니다.

첨부 : 상기 의사록. 끝.

수신처 : 경제기획원장관, 재무부장관, 국방부장관, 내무부장관,
상공부장관, 법무부장관, 건설부장관, 동력자원부장관,
교통부장관, 체신부장관, 노동부장관, 보건사회부장관,
농수산부장관, 공보처장관, 관세청장, 해운항만청장,
산림청장, 철도청장, 서울시장

0176

외교문서 비밀해제: 주한미군지위협정(SOFA) 27
주한미군지위협정(SOFA) 한 · 미 합동위원회 4

초판인쇄 2024년 03월 15일
초판발행 2024년 03월 15일

지은이 한국학술정보(주)
펴낸이 채종준
펴낸곳 한국학술정보(주)
주 소 경기도 파주시 회동길 230(문발동)
전 화 031-908-3181(대표)
팩 스 031-908-3189
홈페이지 http://ebook.kstudy.com
E-mail 출판사업부 publish@kstudy.com
등 록 제일산-115호(2000. 6. 19)

ISBN 979-11-7217-038-7 94340
979-11-7217-011-0 94340 (set)

책에 대한 더 나은 생각, 끊임없는 고민, 독자를 생각하는 마음으로 보다 좋은 책을 만들어갑니다.